DOLL KNITS

DOLL KNITS
Over 40 Patterns to Knit and Crochet

Zazel Lovén and Patricia Ann Higgins

BALLANTINE BOOKS • NEW YORK

Produced for Ballantine Books
by TENTH AVENUE EDITIONS, INC.
Managing Editor: Clive Giboire
Associate Editor: Suzanne Gagné
Art Directors: Walter Skibitsky and B. Dino Marcial
Photographer: Juracek-Old
Doll Illustrations: Deirdre Newman Griffin

Every effort has been made to make the instructions accurate and complete. We cannot be responsible for variance of individual workmanship, human errors or typographical mistakes.

Copyright © 1986 by Zazel Loven and Patricia Ann Higgins

All rights reserved under International and Pan-American Copyright Conventions. Published in the United States by Ballantine Books, a division of Random House, Inc., New York, and simultaneously in Canada by Random House of Canada Limited, Toronto.

Library of Congress Catalog Card Number: 86-90751

ISBN: 0-345-33277-6

Cover design by Richard Aquan
Cover photo by Jan Juracek

Manufactured in the United States of America

First Edition: September 1986
10 9 8 7 6 5 4 3 2 1

CONTENTS

BACK TO SCHOOL
Child's Scottie Sweater, 9
Doll's Scottie Sweater, 10
Color photograph, 17

SCHOOL DAYS—ABC DAYS
Granny's Square Suit, 11
Doll's Pinafore, 12
Tweed Crewneck, 13
Girl's Pinafore, 14
Color photograph, 18 and 19

HAPPY HALLOWEEN!
Bumblebee, 15
Pirate, 16
Teddy Bear, 26
Clown, 27
Color photograph, 20 and 21

WINTER PLAYGROUND
Snowflake Outfit, 28
Winter-Bright Sweater, 29
Irish Knit, 31
Color photograph, 22 and 23

CHRISTMAS CONFECTION
Glitter Sweater, 33
Child's Christmas Crewneck, 34
Doll's Christmas Crewneck, 35
Holiday Ensemble, 36
Color photograph, 24

VALENTINE DELIGHT
Hearts and Stripes, 37
Boy's Heart Pullover, 38
Child's Valentine Cardigan, 38
Dolls Valentine Cardigan, 40
Color photograph, 41

EASTER PARADE
Easter Outfit, 49
Boy's Easter Suit, 50
Flower-Trimmed Dress, 52
Springtime Pinafore, 53
Color photograph, 42 and 43

BRAND-NEW BABY: A PRECIOUS GIFT
Christening Gown, 53
Layette, 55
Color photograph, 44 and 45

SUMMER: TIME FOR FUN
Sailor Girl and Boy, 56
Tennis Set, 57
Jogging Suit, 58
Color photograph, 46 and 47

MIX AND MATCH, 59
Color photograph, 48

HOW TO KNIT, 61

HOW TO CROCHET, 63

ACKNOWLEDGEMENTS

The authors and Tenth Avenue Editions would first like to thank Michelle Russell and Teri Henry of Ballantine Books for their inspiration and encouragement. We are also indebted to Francine Bonica, Peggy Greig, Alexandra Failmezger, Donald Grover, Elizabeth Kodela, Karyn Repinski, Loni Rogers, Barbara Stoecker, and Susan Woodward for their creative input. Thanks are due to Mr. & Mrs. Edgar Wilde for allowing our dolls to use their ski run; to Daybreak Nurseries of Westport, Connecticut, for a breath of spring in deepest winter; to Mr. & Mrs. Thomas Occhiogrosso for our dolls' Christmas party; and to Carol DiGrappa for the dolls' summer vacation. Thanks are also due to Rose Mary Balchi and Jillian Lee Occhiogrosso, little girls who gave the dolls a mother's care. Special thanks are due to the companies that provided dolls for photography: Fruit Kids, Golden Playthings (Huggy Bean Dolls), McCall's Patterns (Blossom Babies), and Simplicity Patterns (Precious Pals); to Bernat Yarn and Craft Corporation for its how-to knit and crochet illustrations.

INTRODUCTION

We welcome you to join us as we wander through the wonderful world of children and their dolls. If you enjoy knitting and crocheting year 'round, you will find something for every season and every holiday. Many of these items can be made by a novice—even a very young one, with some help and encouragement. Add to your special child's fun and fantasy with a gift that goes on and on.

Abbreviations

The following abbreviations and terms were used in this book.

beg .... beginning	yo .... yarn over
dec .... decrease	k .... knit
inc .... increase	p .... purl
lp .... loop	St st .... Stockinette st
pat .... pattern	SKP ... sl 1, k 1, pass slip st over k st
rem .... remaining	ch .... chain
rep .... repeat	sc .... single crochet
sl .... slip	hdc .... half double crochet
sp .... space	dc .... double crochet
st .... stitch	tr .... triple crochet
tog .... together	rnd .... round

*Means repeat the instructions following the * as many times as indicated.

Sometimes you will see a phrase like *[ch 1, skip ch 1, dc in next ch] 2 times*. This means that whatever is included in the bracket should be repeated the number of times specified directly after the closing bracket.

Gauge

The importance of gauge in knitting and crocheting can not be overemphasized. Even the most experienced craftpersons should check their gauge when beginning a new pattern. Make a small sample of your stitches. Put 2 pins exactly 1" apart and count the stitches between. Do the same to count your rows. If you have more stitches or rows to the inch than the pattern, change to a larger needle or hook size. If you have fewer stitches or rows to the inch, change to a smaller needle or hook size.

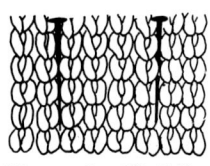 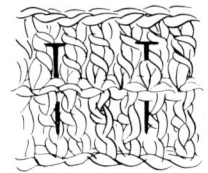

Measuring Knitting   *Measuring Crochet*

Techniques

We have included a basic how-to section on pages 61 through 64, but we want to explain a few stitches or techniques used frequently in this book.

Garter St: K all rows.
Stockenette St: K on right side, p on wrong side.
K 1, P 1 Rib: Worked on an odd number of sts. Row 1 (wrong side): P 1, *k 1, p 1; rep from * across. Row 2: K 1, *p 1, k 1; rep from *

across. Repeat these 2 rows for pattern.

Seed St: Worked on an odd-number of sts. Row 1: K 1, *p 1, k 1; rep from * across. Repeat this row for pat.

To Make a Pompon: Cut two cardboard disks to desired size of pompon; cut out hole nn center of both. Thread needle with double strand of yarn. Place disks together. Cover with yarn, working through holes. Slip scissors between disks. Cut yarn around outside edge. Draw strand of yarn between disks and wind several times very tightly around yarn; knot, leaving ends for attaching pompon. Remove disks; fluff out yarn into a pompon. Trim any uneven ends.

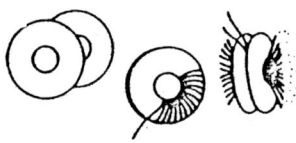

Sizing

Most doll companies size their dolls by height, but this is not a very useful measurement when sizing sweaters! Therefore, we have graded our patterns by the body measurements—measure the doll you are dressing, and choose the appropriate size from the table below. Doll Head sizes also vary greatly, so also measure the head. We found that a medium-size doll could well wear a large-size hat.

Children's sizing is standard in this table.

Doll's Sizes

Measurement	Small	Medium	Large
Actual Chest	12"	14"	16"
Finished Garment	14"	16"	18"
Hat	12½"	14½"	16½"

Children's Sizes

Measurement	2	4	6	8
Chest	21"	23"	25"	27"
Waist	20"	21"	22"	23"
Back Neck to Waist	8½"	9½"	10½"	12½"

BACK TO SCHOOL

Child's Scottie Sweater

Directions are for Size 2. Changes for Sizes 4, 6 and 8 are in parentheses.

MATERIALS: Galler Olympia (50–gr. ball)—2 (3-3-4) balls yellow, 1 ball each red and black. Size 8 knitting needles, OR SIZE REQUIRED TO OBTAIN GAUGE. Size 5 knitting needles.
GAUGE: 5 sts and 7 rows = 1″.

FRONT: With smaller needles and yellow, cast on 65 (71-77-83) sts. Work in k 1, p 1 rib until 11 (13-15-15) rows are completed. Change to larger needles and St st and work 6 (10-0-8) rows even. Mark 6 (7-8-9) sts from each side edge. **Place Argyle:** K in yellow to first marker, following chart in Figure 1, k Row 1 of argyle, work in yellow across until 9 sts before next marker, k Row 1 of argyle, k in yellow to end. Work in pat as established, rep argyle, until Row 10 of 2nd (2nd-3rd-3rd) argyle is completed. Mark center 13 sts. **Next Row:** K in pat to first center marker, following chart in Figure 2, k Row 1 of scottie, k in pat to end. Continue in pat as established until 12 rows of scottie and 3 (3-4-4) argyle pat are completed; at same time, when 9″ (9½″-10½″-11½″), end with p row. **Divide for Neck Opening:** K 25 (27-29-29), with second strand of yellow, k next 15 (17-19-19) sts and sl to holder, work to end. Dec 1 st at each neck edge every other row 4 (4-5-5) times—21 (23-25-27) sts each side. Work even until 1″ above last argyle row. Bind off.

BACK: Cast on and work rib as for front. Change to larger needles and St st and work even until back is same length as front to shoulder. **Shape Shoulders and Neck:** Bind off 21 (23-25-27) sts at beg of next 2 rows; sl rem 23 (25-27-29) sts to holder.

SLEEVES: With smaller needles and yellow, cast on 31 (35-37-41) sts. Work in k 1, p 1, rib for 2″ (2″-3″-3″); end with Row 1. Change to larger needles and St st. Inc 1 st each edge on next row, then every 4th row 14 times more—61 (65-67-71) sts. Work even until 13″ (14″-15″-16″) from beg. Bind off.

FINISHING: Sew left shoulder seam. **Neckband:** Right side facing, with smaller needles and yellow, k sts from back holder, pick up and k about 15 sts to front holder, k sts from front

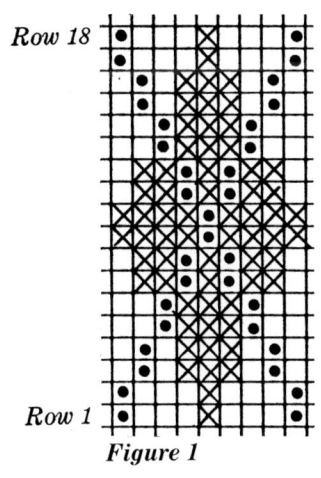

Figure 1

☐ Yellow
⊙ Black
☒ Red

Figure 2

holder, pick up and k about 16 sts to end. Work in k 1, p 1 rib for 1". Bind off.
Sew right shoulder seam. Centering top of sleeve at shoulder seam, sew sleeves in place. Sew side and sleeve seams.

Doll's Scottie Sweater

Directions are for Small. Changes for Medium and Large are in parentheses.

MATERIALS: Galler Pony (50-gr. ball)—1 ball each yellow, black and red. Size 6 knitting needles, OR SIZE REQUIRED TO OBTAIN GAUGE. Size 4 knitting needles. Size D crochet hook. Velcro for back closing.

GAUGE: 6 sts and 8 rows = 1".

FRONT: With smaller needles and yellow, cast on 43 (49-55) sts. Work in k 1, p 1 rib for 5 rows. Change to larger needles and St st and work even for 2 (6-6) rows. Mark 2 (3-4) sts from each side edge. **Place Argyle:** K in yellow to first marker, following chart in Figure 1, k Row 1 of argyle, k in yellow across until 9 sts before next marker, k Row 1 of argyle, k in yellow to end. Keep pat as established until 10th row of argyle pat is completed. Mark center 13 sts. **Next Row:** K in pat to first center marker, following chart in Figure 2, k Row 1 of scottie, k in pat to end. Work in pat until ½" above scottie pat. **Divide for Neck Opening:** Work 13 (15-17) sts, with second strand of yellow, bind off 17 (19-21) sts, work to end. Dec 1 st at each neck edge every other row 3 times—10 (12-15) sts. When 4½" (5½"-6½") from beg, bind off for shoulders.

BACKS: With smaller needles and yellow, cast on 23 (25-27) sts. Work in k 1, p 1 rib as for front. Change to larger needles and work in St st until same length as front. Bind off.

SLEEVES: With smaller needles and yellow, cast on 35 (51-51) sts. Work in k 1, p 1 rib for 5 rows. Change to larger needles and St st. Inc 1 st each edge every 4th row 5 (6-6) times. When 3" (3½"-4") from beg, bind off.

FINISHING: Sew shoulder seams. Centering sleeves at shoulder seams, sew in sleeves. Sew side and sleeve seams. Right side facing, with D hook and yellow, beg at left back edge, work 1 row sc up back, around neck, and down back keeping work flat. Fasten off. Sew Velcro in place.

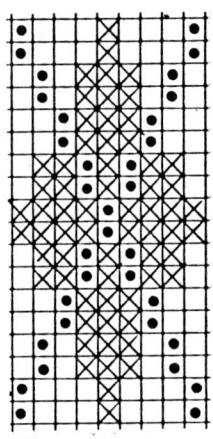

Figure 1

☐ *Yellow*
⊙ *Black*
⊠ *Red*

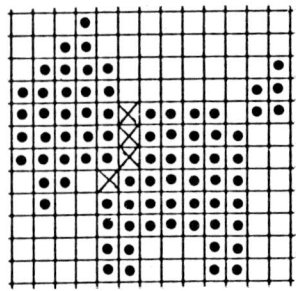

Figure 2

SCHOOL DAYS—ABC DAYS

Granny's Square Suit

Directions are for Small. Changes for Medium and Large are in parentheses.

MATERIALS: Bucilla Spectator (2–oz. skein)—1 each primrose and larkspur. Size E crochet hook, OR SIZE REQUIRED TO OBTAIN GAUGE. Velcro for back closing. 6 small pearl buttons.
GAUGE: 1 square = 1½" (1¾"–1¾"); 9 hdc = 2".

SWEATER
SQUARE: Make 30. With primrose, ch 4; join with sl st to form ring. **Row 1:** Ch 3, 2 dc in ring, ch 2, [3 dc in ring, ch 2] 3 times; join with sl st to 3rd ch of starting ch. Fasten off. **Row 2:** Join larkspur in any ch–2 sp, ch 2 (3–3), 2 hdc (dc–dc) in same sp, ch 2, 3 hdc (dc–dc) in same sp, ch 1, [in next sp, work 3 hdc (dc–dc), ch 2, 3 hdc (dc–dc), ch 1] 3 times; join with sl st to last ch of starting ch.

Sl st to form ring

FINISHING: Whipstitch motifs tog following chart. **Rib:** With primrose, ch 5. **Row 1:** Sc in 2nd ch from hook and each rem ch. **Row 2:** Ch 1, turn; working in back lp only, sc in each sc. Rep Row 2 until long enough to fit bottom edge. Fasten off. Sew in place. Work rib for sleeve in same manner. **Front Bands:** Right side facing, join primrose at neck edge of left front, ch 1, sc in each st to bottom edge. **Row 2:** Ch 3 (counts as first dc), dc in each rem st. **Row 3:** Ch 1, turn; sc in each st. Fasten off. Sew on 6 buttons evenly spaced, with the first ¼" from neck edge and the last ½" from bottom edge. **Right Front Band:** Right side facing, join primrose at bottom edge and work as for left front band, working buttonholes on Row 2 opposite buttons as follows: Work to opposite button, ch 1, skip 1 sc, dc in next sc. **Collar:** With primrose, ch 8. Work in rib as above on 7 sc until long enough to fit neck edge with enough ease to turn down smoothly. Fasten off. Sew Collar in place.

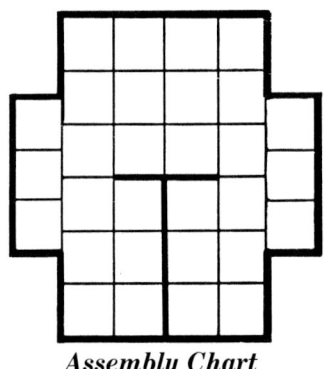
Assembly Chart

SKIRT
With larkspur, ch 66 (74-82). **Row 1:** Hdc in 3rd ch from hook and each rem ch—64 (72-80) hdc. **Row 2:** Ch 2 (counts as first hdc), turn; hdc across. Rep Row 2 until 4" (4½"-5") from beg. **Last Row:** Ch 1, turn; sc in 2nd st, ch 1; skip 1 st, sc in next st, repeat from * across. Fasten off.

FINISHING: Taking care to keep work flat, work 1 row sc along each back edge. **Waist Tie:** Ch about 20" (22"-24"); sl st in 2nd ch and each rem ch. Fasten off. Weave tie through space left by skipped sts on last row. Sew Velcro in place.

LEG WARMERS
Work rib on ch 5 as for sweater's bottom edge for 5" (6"-6"); do not fasten off. Drop primrose; join larkspur. **Row 1:** Turn; working along side of rib, ch 2 (counts as first hdc), hdc in end of each row across. **Row 2:** Ch 2, turn; working in back lp only, hdc in each hdc. Drop larkspur. Working as for Row 2, work [2 rows primrose, 2 rows larkspur] twice. Fasten off. Work rib as for bottom edge. Sew to top. Sew back seam.

Doll's Pinafore

Directions are for Small. Changes for Medium and Large are in parentheses.

MATERIALS: Bucilla Spectator (2–oz. skein)—1 skein. Size 5 knitting needles, OR SIZE REQUIRED TO OBTAIN GAUGE. Size 3 needles. Size D crochet hook. 1 yd. matching ¾" ribbon. Velcro for back closing and strap fastening.
GAUGE: 6 sts and 8 rows = 1".

SKIRT GORE: Make 4. With larger needles, beg at bottom edge, cast on 50 (58-60) sts. K 4 rows for garter st border. Continue in St st, and dec 1 st each edge every 4th row 8 (8-9) times. When 5" (5½"-6") from beg, sl sts to holder.
FINISHING: Weave seams, leaving back seam open. **Top Band:** Right side facing, sl sts to smaller needle. With smaller needles, k 2 tog across. Continue in garter st for 1". Bind off loosely. **Straps:** Cast on 7 sts. Work even in St st for 6" (7"-7"). Bind off. Sew straps to ribbon and sew to front. Work 1 row sc along each side of back opening. Sew Velcro in place to close. Sew Velcro in place to fasten straps to back.

Tweed Crewneck

Directions are for Small. Changes for Medium and Large are in parentheses.

MATERIALS: Bucilla Spectator (2–oz. skein)—1 skein terracotta, small amounts each yellow and

orange. Size E crochet hook, OR SIZE REQUIRED TO OBTAIN GAUGE. Velcro for back closing.

GAUGE: 9 dc = 2″; in Tweed pat, 5 sts = 1″.

TWEED PAT: Row 1 (Right Side): With yellow, carrying terracotta along top of last row and working over it, sc in 1 st, *ch 1, skip 1 st, sc in next st; rep from * across; fasten off yellow. **Row 2:** With terracotta, ch 1, *sc in next ch sp, ch 1; rep from * across. **Row 3:** With orange and carrying terracotta as before, sc in ch–1 sp, *ch 1, sc in ch–1 sp; rep from * across. Fasten off orange. **Row 4:** Rep Row 2. **Row 5:** With yellow and carrying terracotta, rep Row 3; fasten off yellow. Rep Rows 2 through 5 for pat.

FRONT: With terracotta, ch 6, **Rib: Row 1:** Sc in 2nd ch from hook and each rem ch. **Row 2:** Ch 1, turn; working in back lp only, sc in each sc—5 sc. Rep Row 2 until 35 (41-45) rows from beg; do not fasten off. Turn work; working along ends of rows, ch 1, sc in each row—35 (41-45) sc. **Establish Pat:** Ch 1, sc in 3 sc, work Row 1 of Tweed Pat until 3 sts rem, sc in 3 sts. **Row 2:** Ch 1, turn; sc in 3 sc, ch 1, work Row 2 of Tweed Pat across until 4 sc rem, ch 1, sc in last 3 sc. Continue in pat as established, working Tweed Pat in center and 3 sc at each edge in terracotta, until 3″ (4″-4″) from beg; end with Row 3 or 5. **Shape Armhole:** Sl st in 4 sts, sc in next 3 sts, work in pat across until 7 sts from end, sc in 3 sts; do not work in rem sts. **Next Row:** Ch 1, turn; sc in 3 sc, work in pat across until 3 sts rem, sc in 3 sc. Work even in pat until 1½″ (2″-2″) above beg of armhole; end with Tweed Pat Row 2 or 4. **Next Row:** Ch 1, turn; sc in 3 sc, work in 2 more sc in Tweed Pat; do not work rem sts. With terracotta, sl st in first sc, ch 1, sc in ch sp, work in pat to end. Work 2 rows even. Fasten off. Join yarn in 6th st from side edge on last long row, and complete to correspond to first side.

RIGHT BACK: Work rib as for front until 18 (21-23) rows from beg; do not fasten off. Working along side edge, ch 3 (counts as first dc), dc in each row across—18 (21-23) dc. Work in in dc until 3″ (4″-4″) from beg. **Shape Armhole:** Sl st in 5 sts, ch 3, dc in rem dc. Work even until same length as back to shoulder. Fasten off.

LEFT BACK: Work as for Right Back to armhole. **Shape Armhole:** Work across in dc until 4 sts rem; do not work rem sts. Complete as for Right Back.

SLEEVES: With terracotta, ch 6; work rib as for front for 17 (27-27) rows. Working in dc as for back, inc 1 st each edge every row, 3 times. Work even until sleeve measures 4½" (5"-5½") from beg. Fasten off.

FINISHING: Sew shoulder seams; sew in sleeves. Sew side and sleeve seams. Right side facing, beg at left back bottom edge, join terracotta. Taking care to keep work flat, work 1 row sc up back edge, around neck edge and down other back edge. Sew Velcro in place.

Girl's Pinafore

Directions are for Size 2. Changes for Sizes 4, 6 and 8 are in parentheses.

MATERIALS: Bucilla 4–Ply Premium Acrylic (3.5–oz. skein)—2 (2-3-3) skeins. Size 8 knitting needles, OR SIZE REQUIRED TO OBTAIN GAUGE. Size 5 knitting needles. 1 yd. matching ¾" ribbon. 2 heavy snaps.

GAUGE: 9 sts and 13 rows = 2".

SKIRT GORE: Make 4. With larger needles, beg at bottom edge, cast on 64 (68-72-76) sts. K 8 rows for garter st border. Continue in St st for 2". Dec 1 st each edge on next row, then every 1" (1"-1½"-2") times more—50 (54-58-62) sts. Work even until 11" (12"-14"-16") from beg. Sl sts to holder.

FINISHING: Weave seams, leaving back seam open. **Top Band:** Right side facing, sl sts to smaller needle. With smaller needle, k 2 tog across. Continue in garter st until 2½" are completed. Bind off loosely. Sew back seam. **Straps:** With smaller needles, cast on 7 sts. Work even in St st until 9½" (10"-10½"-11") from beg. Bind off. (**Note:** If desired, straps can be made longer; then, as the girl grows taller, by moving a snap, the pinafore can grow into a suspender skirt.) Sew straps in place on front; sew snaps on ends and on back.

HAPPY HALLOWEEN!

Bumblebee

Directions are for Small. Changes for Medium and Large are in parentheses.

MATERIALS: Coats & Clark Red Heart Sport Yarn (2–oz. skein)—1 each black and yellow. Size E crochet hook, OR SIZE REQUIRED TO OBTAIN GAUGE. Velcro for back closing. Fine black wire.

GAUGE: 5 dc = 1″; 5 rows = 2″.

LEFT BACK: With black, ch 18 (20-22). **Row 1:** Dc in 4th ch from hook and each rem ch—16 (18-20) dc. **Row 2:** Ch 3 (counts as first dc), dc in 2nd dc and each rem dc. **Next Row (Inc Row):** Ch 3, turn; dc in same st, work dc across, 2 dc in last dc. Continue in dc; rep inc row every other row 1 (2-2) more times—20 (24-26) dc. Work even until 3″ from beg. **Shape Crotch:** Sl st in 3 dc, ch 3, dec 1 dc over next 2 dc, work in dc across. **Next Row:** Work across until 3 sts rem, dec 1 dc over next 2 dc, dc in last st—16 (20-22) dc. Work even until 1½″ (2″-2″) above beg of crotch shaping. Drop black; join yellow. Work [2 rows yellow, 2 rows black] twice and 2 rows yellow. Fasten off yellow. Continue with black until 9″ (10″-10″) from beg. Fasten off.

RIGHT BACK: Work as for left back, reversing shaping.

FRONT: Work legs as for right and left back until 1 row after crotch shaping is complete. Tack last row tog at crotch seam. **Joining Row:** Work across first leg, continue in dc across second leg—32 (40-44) dc. Continue in dc, working color stripes to match backs; at the same time, when 8″ (9″-9″), end at side edge. **Shape Neck:** Mark center 24 (30-34) sts. **Next Row:** Work until 3 sts before marked st, dec 1 st over next 2 sts, dc in last st. Work even until same length as back. Fasten off. Join yarn in next marked st on last full row, ch 3, dec 1 dc over next 2 dc, work to end. Work even until same length as back. Fasten off.

SLEEVES: With black, ch 28 (32-32). Work 1 row as for back—26 (30-30) dc. Inc 1 st each edge every other row twice. Work even on 30 (34-34) dc until 8 (9-10) rows from beg. Fasten off.

WINGS: (**Note:** When working Rows 1, 3, 5, 7 and 9, hold wire along ch and work sc over wire, covering it. Cut wire at end of row. Bend ends back into work, covering them.) With yellow, ch 17. **Row 1:** Sc in 2nd ch from hook and each rem ch. **Row 2:** *Ch 7, sk 3 sc, sc in next sc; rep from * across. **Row 3:** Ch 1, turn; *9 sc in ch sp, sc in sc; rep from * across. **Row 4:** Sl st in first 4 sts; *ch 10, sk 9 sts, sc in next st; rep from * across; sl st in next st. **Row 5:** Ch 1, turn; *12 sc in ch sp, sc in sc; rep from * across. **Row 6:** Ch 1, turn; sl st in 6 sts, *ch 10, sk 5 sts, sc in 3 sts, ch 10, sk 5 sts, sc in next st; rep from * once; ch 10, sk 5 sts, sc in next st. **Row 7:** Ch 2, turn; *12 sc in ch sp, sc in sc; rep from * across. **Row 8:** Ch 1, turn; sl st in first 6 sts, *ch 1 [ch 15, sc in center st of next sp] twice; turn. **Row 9:** Ch 1, [17 sc in ch sp, sl st in sc] twice. Fasten off. Sew wings to back as shown.

HAT: With black, ch 75. **Row 1:** Dc in 4th ch from hook and each rem ch. **Row 2:** Ch 3 (counts as first dc), dc in each dc across; drop black; join yellow. **Row 3:** With yellow, rep Row 2. Drop yellow. **Row 4:** With black, ch 3, *dec 1 dc over next 2 dc, dc in next dc; rep from * across. **Row 5:** Rep Row 2; drop black. **Row 6:** With yellow, rep Row 2; cut yellow. **Row 7:** With black, rep Row 4. **Row 8:** Rep Row 2. **Row 9:** Rep Row 4—21 sts. Cut black, leaving a 15" end. Thread end through top of last row and draw up tightly; sew back seam.

ANTENNAE: With black, ch 30. Working over wire as for wings, 2 sc in 2nd ch from hook and each rem ch. Fasten off. Bend into a tight spiral. Sew in place as shown.

FINISHING: Sew backs to fronts until beg of crotch shaping; seam front tog from crotch to joining; sew backs tog from beg of crotch to first yellow stripe. Sew shoulder seams. Centering sleeves at shoulder seam, sew sleeves in place. Sew side and sleeve seams. Join black at bottom of back opening, work 1 row sc up back, around neck edge, and down other back, taking care to keep work flat. Fasten off. Sew Velcro in place to close back.

Pirate

Directions are for Small. Changes for Medium and Large are in parentheses.

MATERIALS: Coats & Clark Red Heart Sport

Continued on page 25

BACK TO SCHOOL

Having your best doll friend dressed just like you makes those first school days lots more fun.

SCHOOL DAYS—ABC DAYS
Happy students make the day brighter for our "pretend" teacher.

WINTER PLAYGROUND

Cheering from the sidelines or joining in the fun—your dolls will be the best dressed for any winter sport!

CHRISTMAS CONFECTION

Share the special meaning of the holiday season with favorite dolls.

Continued from page 16

Yarn (2–oz. skein)—1 oz. each blue, red, white and yellow. Size 5 knitting needles, OR SIZE REQUIRED TO OBTAIN GAUGE. Velcro for back closing. Black heavy cardboard for sword and eye patch. Small amt silver craft paint. 1 ft black hat elastic. ½ yd. 2½" Offray red satin ribbon. Bandanna or similar fabric.

GAUGE: 6 sts and 8 rows = 1".

SUIT

LEFT BACK: With blue, cast on 19 (21-25) sts. Work 3 rows Seed st for bottom band. Continue in St st, inc 1 st each edge every 6th row, 3 (4-4) times—25 (29-33) sts. Work even until 3½" from beg. **Shape Crotch:** Bind off 2 sts at beg of next row, then dec 1 st at same edge every other row 2 (3-4) times—21 (23-27) sts. Work even until 5" from beg. Fasten off blue. Continue in Stripe Pat [6 rows red, 6 rows white] until 7½" from beg; end at side edge. **Shape Armhole:** Bind off 3 sts at beg of next row. Work even until 3" (3½"-3½") above beg of armhole. Bind off.

RIGHT BACK: Work as for left back, reversing crotch and armhole shaping.

RIGHT FRONT: Work as for left back until 1" less than back to shoulder; end at crotch edge. **Shape Neck:** Bind off 6 (7-8) sts at beg of next row, then dec 1 st every k row 3 times. When same length as back bind off.

LEFT FRONT: Work as for right front, reversing shaping.

SLEEVES: With red, cast on 35 (39-39) sts. Work 3 rows Seed st. Continue in St st and Stripe Pat until 3½" (4"-4") from beg. Bind off.

FINISHING: Sew fronts tog from neck to crotch; bind off. Sew fronts to back at shoulder seams; sew fronts to backs from crotch to bottom. Sew back seam from crotch to first red stripe. Centering sleeves at shoulder seams, sew in place, sewing bound-off edges of armhole to sides of sleeves. Sew sleeve and side seams. Beg at bottom of back opening, work 1 row sc up back, around neck and down other side, taking care to keep work flat. Sew Velcro in place.

VEST

BACK: With yellow, cast on 45 (49-53) sts. Work 3 rows Seed st. Continue in St st until 2" from beg. **Next Row:** Work 6 sts Seed st, continue across in St st until 6 sts rem, work Seed st to end. Work 2 more rows the same.

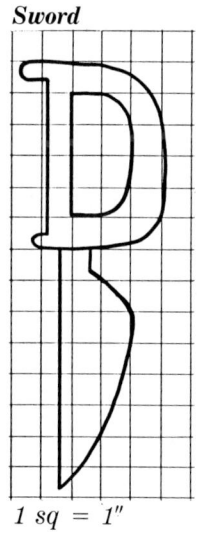

Sword

1 sq = 1"

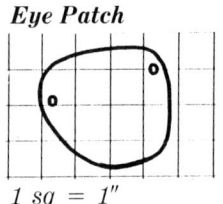

Eye Patch

1 sq = 1"

Shape Armhole: Bind off 3 sts at beg of next 2 rows. Keeping 3 sts at each armhole edge in Seed st, continue in St st until 3½" (4"-4") above beg of armhole. Bind off.

RIGHT FRONT: With yellow, cast on 21 (23-25) sts. Work 3 rows Seed st. **Next Row:** Work 3 sts in Seed st, k across. Continue in St st, keeping 3 sts at front edge in Seed st until 2" from beg; end at side edge. **Next Row:** Work 6 sts Seed st, St st across until 3 sts rem, seed st on 3 sts.

Shape Neck and Armhole: Seed st on 3 sts, SKP, work across to last 6 sts, Seed st to end. Bind off 3 sts at beg of next row; work across in pat. Keeping 3 sts at side edge in Seed st, dec 1 st inside front Seed st border every other row 6 (7-8) more times. Work even until same length as back to shoulder. Bind off.

LEFT FRONT: Work as for right front reversing shaping.

FINISHING: Sew shoulder and side seams of vest.

Sword and Eye Patch: Enlarge patterns to size. Cut cardboard. Paint handle of sword with silver. Make 2 holes in eye patch and thread elastic through. Tie around doll's head. Cut triangle of fabric and tie in place. Tie ribbon around waist, and slide sword into place.

Teddy Bear

Directions are for Small. Changes for Medium and Large are in parentheses.

MATERIALS: Coats & Clark Red Heart Sport Yarn (2–oz. skein)—2 skeins brown, small amt pink. Size 5 knitting needles, OR SIZE REQUIRED TO OBTAIN GAUGE. Size E hook. Velcro for back closing.

GAUGE: 6 sts and 8 rows = 1".

SUIT: With brown, work as for Pirate Suit.

HAT: Cast on 51 (61-71) sts. Work in Seed st for 3 rows. Keeping 3 sts at each side edge in Seed st, continue in St st for 2½" (3"-3½"). **Shape Back:** Bind off 17 (20-24) sts at beg of next 2 rows. Work even in St st until 2¼" (2½-2¾") from bind off. Work 3 rows Seed st. Bind off.

Ears: With E hook and brown, ch 7. **Row 1:** 2 sc in 2nd ch from hook, sc in 4 ch, 2 sc in last ch. **Row 2:** Ch 1, turn; 2 sc in first sc, sc across until last st, 2 sc in last st. **Row 3:** Rep Row 2. **Row**

4: Ch 1, turn; dec 1 sc over first 2 sc, work across until 2 sc rem, dec 1 sc over last 2 sc. Rep Row 4 twice. Fasten off. **Inside:** With pink, ch 2. **Rnd 1:** 6 sc in 2nd ch from hook; join with sl st to first sc. **Rnd 2:** Ch 1, 2 sc in each sc around; join. Fasten off. Sew inside to center of ear. Sew ears to hat 8 rows from front edge as shown. Sew bound-off edges of back shaping to side edges of back, easing to fit. **Ties:** Ch 12". Sl st in 2nd ch from hook and each rem ch. Sew to each end of cast-on row.

Clown

Directions are for Small. Changes for Medium and Large are in parentheses.

MATERIALS: Coats & Clark Red Heart Sport Yarn (2–oz. skein)—1 oz. each yellow, green, pink, blue and red. Size 5 knitting needles, OR SIZE REQUIRED TO OBTAIN GAUGE. Size E crochet hook. Velcro for back closing. 2 La Mode star-shaped buttons.

GAUGE: 6 sts and 8 rows = 1".

LEFT BACK: With pink, cast on 57 (63-75) sts. Work 3 rows Seed st. Continue in St st until 1" from beg; end wrong side row. **Next Row:** K 3 tog across—19 (21-25) sts. Working in pink throughout, complete as for Pirate, beg after Seed st bottom band.

RIGHT BACK: With blue, work as for Left Back, reversing shaping.

LEFT FRONT: With yellow, cast on and work as for right back. Shape neck as for left front of pirate.

RIGHT FRONT: With green, work as for left front reversing shaping.

SLEEVES: Make 1 pink and 1 yellow. Cast on 105 (117-117) sts and work as for left back for 1". **Next Row:** K 3 tog across. Work even in St st until 3½" (4"-4") from beg. Bind off.

FINISHING: Sew tog as for Pirate, leaving about 6" open at back. With blue, work sc row around back opening and neck to finish. **Collar.** Right side facing, (with blue) beg at left back neck edge, pick up 3 sts in each sc around. Beg with k row, work in St st until ¾" from beg. Work 3 rows Seed st. Bind off loosely.

Front Trim: Make 1 pink and 1 red. Work as for inside ear of Teddy Bear. Sew to front as shown, sew button in middle.

WINTER PLAYGROUND

Snowflake Outfit

Directions are for Small. Changes for Medium and Large are in parentheses.

MATERIALS: Patons Solo (50–gr. ball)—2 balls blue, 1 ball each rose and white. Size 5 knitting needles, OR SIZE REQUIRED TO OBTAIN GAUGE. Size 3 needles. Velcro to close sweater back.
GAUGE: 6 sts and 7 rows = 1″.

SWEATER
FRONT: With smaller needles and blue, cast on 39 (45-51) sts. Work in k 1, p 1 rib for 7 rows. Change to larger needles. **Pat Row 1:** k 1 blue, *k 1 white, k 1 blue; rep from * across (see Chart I). **Row 2:** P 1 blue, *p 1 white, p 1 blue; rep from * across. With rose, k 1 row, p 1 row. **Rows 5 and 6:** Rep Rows 1 and 2. Fasten off rose and white. With blue, work 6 (10-12) rows St st. Continue in St st, following Chart II; beg and end pat as indicated; keep 1 (4-1) st at each edge in blue. When chart is completed, mark center 23 (27-31) sts. Fasten off rose and white.
Shape Neck and Shoulders: With blue, work to first marker, join 2nd strand of yarn and work to next marker; sl sts to holder for neck; work to end. Working each side separately, dec 1 st at each neck edge on next row, then every row twice more. Bind off.
BACKS: With smaller needles and blue, cast on 19 (23-25) sts. Work in ribbing as for front. Change to larger needles and work even in St st until same length as back to shoulder. Bind off.
SLEEVES: With smaller needles and blue, cast on 37 (49-49) sts. Work in rib as for front. Change to larger needles and St st, inc 1 st each edge every 4th row 6 (7-7) times. When 3″ (3½″-4″) from beg, bind off.
FINISHING: Sew shoulder seams. Centering sleeves at shoulder seam, sew sleeves in place. Sew side and sleeve seams. With smaller needles and blue, pick up and k about 65 (69-73) sts around neck edge, including sts from holder. Bind off. With smaller needles and blue, pick up and k about 34 (38-40) sts along back edge. Bind off. Work other side the same. Sew Velcro in place to close back.

Figure 1

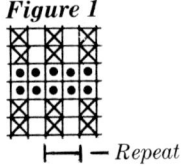

— *Repeat*

Figure 2

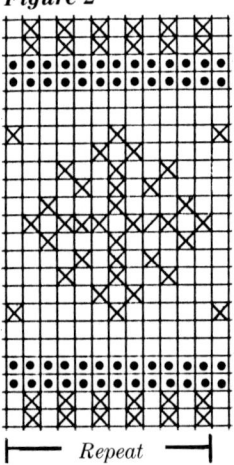

— *Repeat* —

☐ *Blue*
⦿ *White*
☒ *Rose*

LEG WARMERS
With smaller needles and blue, cast on 39 sts. Work k 1, p 1 rib for 5 rows. Change to larger needles and work in St st for 4 rows. Work in pattern following Chart I for 6 rows. With blue, work 6 rows St st. Work 6 rows pat following Chart I. Fasten off white and rose. Work 4 more rows St st. Change to smaller needles and work 5 rows rib as before. Bind off. Sew back seams.

HAT
With smaller needles and blue, cast on 73 (85-97) sts. Work in rib as for back. Change to larger needles and St st, and work in pat following Chart II, having 6 (7-8) pat rep. When chart is completed, work even until 5″ from beg. **1st Dec Row:** K 1, *k 2 tog, k 10; rep from * across. Work 3 rows St st. **2nd Dec Row:** K 1, *k 2 tog, k 9; rep from * across. Work 3 rows St st. Continue in this manner, dec 6 (7-8) sts every 4th row, having 1 less st between decs on each dec row, until 13 (15-17) sts rem. Work Rows 1 and 2 from Chart I. Fasten off blue and white. With rose, k 1, *k 2 tog; rep from * across. **Last Row:** [P 2 tog] 3 (4-4) times, p 1 (0-1). Cut yarn, leaving a 12″ end. Thread yarn through rem sts and fasten securely. Sew back seam, matching pats.

Winter Bright Sweater

Directions are for Small. Changes for Medium and Large are in parentheses.

MATERIALS: Patons Promise (40–gr. ball)—1 ball each orange, yellow, pink and green. Size E crochet hook, OR SIZE REQUIRED TO OBTAIN GAUGE.
GAUGE: 5 dc = 1″; 5 rows = 2″.

SWEATER
RIGHT BACK: With orange, ch 5. **Rib: Row 1:** Sc in 2nd ch from hook and each rem ch. **Row 2:** Ch 1, turn; working in back 1p only, sc in each sc—4 sc. Rep Row 2 until 17 (21-23) rows from beg; do not fasten off. Turn work; working along ends of rows, ch 1, sc in each row—17 (21-23) sts. Fasten off orange. Join yellow; ch 3 (counts as first dc), dc in each rem st. Continue to work even until 3″ (4″-4″) from beg. **Shape Armhole:** Sl st in 6 sts, ch 3, dc across—12 (16-18) sts. Work even until 3″ (3½″-3½″) above beg of armhole. Fasten off.

LEFT BACK: Work same as right back to armhole. **Shape Armhole:** Work in dc across until 5 sts rem; do not work rem sts. Complete as for right back.

FRONT: With yellow, work rib as for back for 35 (43-47) rows. Turn work; work 1 row sc along ends of rows. Fasten off yellow. Join orange and continue in dc on 35 (43-47) sts until 2 rows less than back to armhole. Mark center 5 sts. **Shape Neck and Armhole:** Work across until 2 sts before marker, dec 1 dc over next 2 sts; do not work rem sts. **Next Row:** Ch 2, turn; dc in next st (ch 2 counts as 1 st dec), dc across. **Next Row:** Sl st in 6 sts, ch 3, dc across until 2 sts from neck edge, dec 1 dc over next 2 dc. Continue to dec 1 st at neck edge every row until 2 (5-7) sts rem. When same length as back to shoulder, fasten off. Sk 5 sts on last long row worked; join orange in next st and work to correspond to first side, reversing shaping.

SLEEVES: Make 1 pink with green rib, and 1 green with pink rib. Work rib as for back for 17 (27-27) rows. Working in dc, inc 1 st each edge every row 3 times. Work even until sleeve measures 4½" (5"-5") from beg. Fasten off.

FINISHING: Sew shoulder seams; sew in sleeves. Sew side and sleeve seams. **Neck Ribbing:** With yellow, ch 5. Work in rib as for back until long enough to fit along 1 side of neck edge from skipped sts to center back. Sew in place. With yellow, work 1 row sc along edges of back. Sew Velcro in place to close back.

HAT

With yellow, ch 4. **Rnd 1:** 5 dc in 4th ch from hook; join with sl st to 3rd ch of starting ch—6 dc. Drop yellow; join orange. **Rnd 2:** Ch 3, dc in same st, 2 dc in each rem dc—12 dc. Drop orange; join green. **Rnd 3:** Ch 3, dc in same st, dc in next st; *2 in next dc, dc in next dc; rep from * around. Drop green; join pink. **Rnd 4:** Ch 3, dc in same st, dc in next 2 dc, *2 dc in next st, dc in next 2 sts; rep from * around. Continue in this manner, having 1 more dc between incs, and working in same color sequence, until 8 rows are completed. **Next Row (Dec Row):** With yellow, ch 3, *dec 1 dc over next 2 sts, dc in 6 dc; rep from * around; end last rep dc in 5 dc; join. Work 2 more rnds keeping to color sequence and dec 6 sts around, having 1 less st between decs on each rnd. Fasten off.

SCARF

With green, ch 18. **Row 1:** Dc in 4th ch from hook and each rem ch. **Row 2:** Ch 3 (counts as first dc), dc in each rem dc—16 dc. Working as for Row 2, work [2 rows orange, 2 rows yellow, 2 rows pink, 2 rows green] 5 times. Fasten off.

Irish Knit

Directions are for Small. Changes for Medium and Large are in parentheses.

MATERIALS: Patons Arran (50–gr. ball)—4 balls. Size 7 knitting needles, OR SIZE REQUIRED TO OBTAIN GAUGE. Size 5 knitting needles. Velcro for back closing. Cable needle. Size E crochet hook.

GAUGE: 9 sts and 10 rows = 1″.

SWEATER

PAT STS: Seed St: Row 1: K 1, * p 1, k 1; rep from * across. Rep Row 1 for pat.

Right Cable: Row 1: Sl 2 sts to cable needle and hold in back, k next 2 sts, k 2 sts from cable needle. **Row 2:** P. **Row 3:** K. **Row 4:** P. Rep these 4 rows for pat.

Left Cable: Row 1: sl 2 sts to cable needle and hold in front, k next 2 sts, k 2 sts from cable needle. **Row 2:** P. **Row 3:** K. **Row 4:** P. Rep these 4 rows for pat.

Diamond Panel: Row 1: P 5, Right Cable over 4 sts, p 5. **Rows 2, 4 and 6:** K the k sts and p the p sts as they face you. **Row 3:** P 4, Right Twist over next 3 sts as follows: sl 1 st to cable needle and hold in back, k next 2 sts, k st from cable needle; Left Twist over next 3 sts as follows: sl 2 sts to cable needle and hold in front, k next st, k 2 sts from cable needle; p 4. **Row 5:** P 3, Right Twist, p 2, Left Twist, p 3. **Row 7:** P 2, Right Twist, p 4, Left Twist, p 2. **Row 8:** K 2, p 2, k 2, k and p in next st (1 st inc), k 3, p 2, k 2. **Row 9:** P 2, k 2, p 3, work Popcorn in next st as follows: k, p, k, p, k all in next st; turn, p 5 sts; turn, k 5 sts; turn, p 5 tog; turn, sl st to right needle; continuing across row, p 3, k 2, p 2. **Row 10:** K 2, p 2, k 3, k 2 tog, k 2, p 2, k 2. **Row 11:** P 2, Left Twist, p 4, Right Twist, p 2. **Rows 12 and 14:** K the k sts and p the p sts as they face you. **Row 13:** P 3, Left Twist, p 2, Right Twist, p 3. **Row 15:** P 4, Left Twist, Right Twist, p 4. **Row 16:** K 5, p 4, k 5. Rep these 16 rows for pat.

FRONT: With smaller needles, cast on 39 (43-47) sts. Work 7 rows k 1, p 1 rib, inc 1 st at end of last row—40 (44-48) sts. Change to larger needles. **Pat Row 1 (Establish Pats):** Seed st over 7 (9-11) sts, p 2, Right Cable over 4 sts, Diamond Panel over 14 sts, Left Cable over 4 sts, p 2, Seed st to end. **Row 2:** Seed st over 7 (9-11) sts, k 2, p 4, k 5, p 4, k 5, p 4, k 2, Seed st to end. Work even in pats as established until 2 full Diamond Panels are complete. **Shape Neck:** Mark center 14 (16-18) sts. Work in pat to first marker, with 2nd strand, bind off sts to next marker, work in pats to end. Dec 1 st each edge every row 4 times, discontinuing pats as necessary. Work even on 9 (10-11) sts until 1½" above beg of neck. Bind off for shoulder.

BACKS: With smaller needles, cast on 19 (21-23) sts, and work in rib as for back. Change to larger needles and Seed st and work even until same length as back to shoulder. Bind off.

SLEEVES: With smaller needles, cast on 25 (29-29) sts and work k 1, p 1 rib for 5 rows. Change to larger needles and Seed st and inc 1 st each edge every 4th row 4 times, working inc sts into pat. When 3" (3½"-4") from beg, bind off.

FINISHING: Sew shoulder seams. Centering sleeves at seam, sew in sleeves. Sew side and sleeve seams. Right side facing, with E hook, beg at left back edge, work 1 row sc up back edge, around neck edge, and down other back, taking care to keep work flat. Fasten off. Sew Velcro in place to close back.

SCARF

With larger needles, cast on 16 sts. Work even in garter st for 26". Bind off.

HAT

With larger needles, cast on 54 (60-66) sts. Work even in garter st for 3". **1st Dec Row:** *K 2 tog, k 4; rep from * across. K 1 row. **2nd Dec Row:** *K 2 tog; k 3; rep from * across. K 1 row. Continue in this manner having 1 less st between decs until 18 (20-22) sts rem. K 2 tog across. Cut yarn leaving a 12" end. Thread end through rem 9 (10-11) sts and fasten securely. Sew back seam.

CHRISTMAS CONFECTION

Glitter Sweater

Directions are for Small. Changes for Medium and Large are in parentheses.

MATERIALS: Pingouin Luciole (20-gr. ball)—1 ball gold. Size E crochet hook, OR SIZE REQUIRED TO OBTAIN GAUGE. Velcro for back closing.

GAUGE: 6 dc and 3 rows = 1".

SPECIAL ABBREVIATIONS: Fdc: Yo and insert hook from front around post of next dc (see Figure 1), yo and draw lp through, [yo and through 2 lps] twice. **Bdc:** Yo and insert hook from back around post of next dc (see Figure 2), yo and draw lp through, [yo and draw through 2 lps] twice.

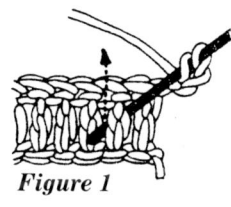

Figure 1

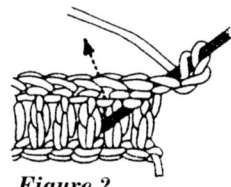

Figure 2

BACKS: Ch 25 (27-29). **Rib: Foundation Row:** Dc in 4th ch from hook and each rem ch—23 (25-27) dc. **Row 1 (wrong side):** Ch 2 (counts as first st), Bdc around next st, *Fdc around next st, Bdc around next st; rep from * across; end with hdc in last st. **Row 2:** Ch 2, Fdc around next st; *Bdc around next st, Fdc around next st; rep from * around; end with hdc in last st. Rep Row 1 once. Continue until 6" from beg. Fasten off.

FRONT: Ch 45 (51-57). Work in rib as for backs on 43 (49-55) sts. Work 1 row dc. First **Popcorn Row:** Mark center st. Work to marked st, work Popcorn in marked st as follows: work 5 dc in same st, drop rem lp from hook, insert hook from front to back through first dc, catch dropped lp and draw through, ch 1 to close; continue in dc to end. Work 1 row dc. **2nd Popcorn Row:** Mark center 7 sts. Work to first marked st, Popcorn, dc in 5 sts, Popcorn, dc to end. Work 1 row dc. **3rd Popcorn Row:** Mark center 13 sts. Work to first marked st, Popcorn, [dc in 5 dc, Popcorn] twice, dc to end. Work 1 row dc. Continue in this manner, having 1 more Popcorn every Popcorn row, with 5 dc between Popcorns, until 6th Popcorn Row is completed. Work 1 row dc. 7th Popcorn Row: Rep 5th Popcorn Row. **Divide for Neck:** Dc in first 11 (13-15) dc, dec 1 dc over next 2 sts; turn. Working 1 side only, dec 1 dc at neck edge 2 times more. When same length as back to shoulder, fasten off. Skip 17 (19-21) sts on last long row worked; join yarn in next st and complete to correspond to first side.

SLEEVES: Ch 31 (47-47). Dc in 4th ch from hook and each rem ch—29 (45-45) dc. Inc 1 st each edge on next row, then every other row 2 times more. When 7 (9-9) rows frm beg, fasten off.

FINISHING: Sew shoulder seams. Centering sleeves at shoulder, sew in sleeves. Sew side and sleeve seams. Taking care to keep work flat, join yarn at bottom left back edge, work 1 row sc up back, around neck and down right back. Fasten off. Sew Velcro in place to close back.

Child's Christmas Crewneck

Directions are for Size 2. Changes for Sizes 4, 6 and 8 are in parentheses.

MATERIALS: Pingouin Pingofrance (50–gr. ball)—ball white and 2 (3-3-4) balls green. Size 5 knitting needles, OR SIZE REQUIRED TO OBTAIN GAUGE. Size 3 knitting needles. 18 Wrights Stick-On Appliqués.

GAUGE: 5 sts and 7 rows = 1″.

BACK: With smaller needles and green, cast on 65 (71-77-83) sts. Work in k 1, p 1 rib for 2″. Change to larger needles and St st and work even until 7″ (8″-9″-10″) from beg or desired length to underarm; end with p row. Fasten off green. **Yoke: Row 1:** K 1 white, *sl 1 with yarn in back, k 1; rep from * across. Continue in St st and white until 4½″ (5″-5½″-6″) from beg of yoke. Bind off.

FRONT: Work as for back until 2″ (2½″-2½″-3″) less than back to bind off; end with p row. **Shape Neck:** K 25 (27-29-31) sts, with 2nd strand of white k next 15 (17-19-21) sts and sl to holder, k to end. Working each side separately, dec 1 st at each neck every row 4 (4-5-5) times. When same length as back to shoulder, bind off.

SLEEVES: With smaller needles and green, cast on 31 (35-37-41) sts. Work in k 1, p 1 rib for 3″. Change to larger needles and St st and inc 1 st each edge every 4th row 14 times more—61 (65-67-71) sts. When 12″ (13″-14″-15″) from beg, bind off.

FINISHING: Sew left shoulder seam. Right side facing, with smaller needles and green, pick up and k about 69 (73-79-83) sts around neck edge including sts from holder. Work in k 1, p 1 rib for 1″. Bind off.

Sew right shoulder seam. Centering sleeve at

seam, sew in sleeves. Sew side and sleeve seams. Place appliqués on yoke as shown (back is same as front); tack in place if desired.

Doll's Christmas Crewneck

Directions are for Small. Changes for Medium and Large are in parentheses.

MATERIALS: Pingouin Pingofrance (50–gr. ball)—1 ball each green and white. Size 3 knitting needles, OR SIZE REQUIRED TO OBTAIN GAUGE. Size 2 knitting needles. Size E crochet hook. 3 Wrights Stick-On Appliqués. Velcro for back closing.
GAUGE: 6 sts and 8 rows = 1″.

BACKS: With smaller needles and green, cast on 23 (25-27) sts. Work in k 1, p 1 rib for 5 rows. Change to larger needles and St st and work even until 3″ (4″-4″) from beg; end wrong side row. Fasten off green. **Yoke:** With white, k 1, *sl 1 with yarn in back, k 1; rep from * across.
Next Row: P. Continue in St st in white until 3″ (4″-4″) above beg of yoke. Fasten off.
FRONT: With smaller needles and green, cast on 43 (49-55) sts and work as for back until 1½″ (2″-2″) above beg of yoke. **Shape Neck:** Work 13 (15-17) sts, with 2nd strand of white, bind off next 17 (19-21) sts, work to end. Dec 1 st at each neck edge every other row 3 times—10 (12-14) sts. When same length as back to shoulder, bind off.
SLEEVES: With smaller needles and green, cast on 35 (41-41) sts. Work in k 1, p 1 rib for 5 rows. Change to larger needles and St st; inc 1 st each edge every 4th row 4 (5-5) times. When 3″ (3½″-4″) from beg, bind off.
FINISHING: Sew shoulder seams. Centering sleeves at shoulder seams, sew in sleeves. Sew side and sleeve seams. Right side facing, with E hook and green, beg at left back edge, work 1 row sc up back, around neck, and down back, taking care to keep work flat. Fasten off. **Neckband:** Right side facing, with smaller needles and green, pick up and k 1 st in each sc around neck edge. Work 3 rows k 1, p 1 rib. Bind off. Apply appliqués to yoke; tack in place if desired. Sew Velcro in place to close back.

Holiday Ensemble

Directions are for Small. Changes for Medium and Large are in parentheses.
MATERIALS: Pingouin Pingofrance (50–gr. ball)—3 balls red, 1 ball white. Size G crochet hook, OR SIZE REQUIRED TO OBTAIN GAUGE. Velcro for back closing.
GAUGE: 7 hdc = 2″.

DRESS
YOKE: With red, ch 46 (54-60). Hdc in 2nd ch from hook and each rem ch—45 (53-59) sts. **Row 2:** Ch 1, turn; hdc in each hdc. Rep Row 2, 0(1-1) times. **Divide for Backs and Front:** Ch 1, turn; hdc in 9 (10-12) sts for back; do not work in rem sts. Ch 1, turn; dec 1 hdc over first 2 sts, hdc across. **Next Row:** Ch 1, turn; hdc in 6 (7-9) sts, dec over next 2 sts. Work even on 7 (8-10) hdc until 7 (8-8) rows above dividing row; fasten off. Skip 5 (6-6) sts on last long row worked, join yarn in next st; ch 1, hdc in same st and next 16 (20-22) sts for front. Work even on 17 (21-23) sts until 4 (6-6) rows in all are worked. **Shape Straps:** Ch 1, turn; hdc in 3 sts. Ch 1, turn, hdc in 3 sts. Work even until strap is 8 rows long. Fasten off. Sk 11 (15-17) sts on front. Join yarn in next st and work 2nd strap to correspond. Sk 5 (6-6) sts on last long row worked; join yarn in next st; complete 2nd back to correspond to first.
SKIRT: Right side facing, join white at bottom left back edge, taking care to keep work flat, work 1 row sc around entire edge to bottom of right back; ch 1, working along opposite side of ch, continue across bottom edge in hdc, inc 9 (10-10) sts evenly spaced across—54 (63-69) sts. Fasten off white. Turn work; join red in last st. Working in back lp only, 2 hdc in each dc across—108 (126-138) hdc. Work even in hdc for 10 (12-12) rows more. Fasten off.
FINISHING: Sew back seam of skirt. Sew Velcro in place to close yoke and fasten straps to back.

CAPE
With red, ch 36. **Row 1:** Hdc in 2nd ch from hook; *2 hdc in next ch, hdc in next ch; rep from * across—52 sts.
Hdc 1 row. **Row 3:** Ch 1, turn; hdc in 2 sts, * 2 hdc in next st, hdc in 3 sts; rep from * across; end last rep hdc in 2 sts–64 sts. Hdc 1 row. **Row 5:** Rep Row 3–80 sts. Hdc 1 row. Rep last 2 rows 2 times more—125 sts. Fasten off red; join

white. **Last Row:** Ch 4, tr in same st; 2 tr in each st across. Fasten off.
FINISHING: Join white at neck edge; working along opposite side of ch, sc in each ch; fasten off. **Tie:** Ch 100. Fasten off. Weave tie through first row of cape. Sew 1" pompon to each end.

VALENTINE DELIGHT

Hearts and Stripes

Directions are for Small. Changes for Medium and Large are in parentheses.

MATERIALS: Bernat Berella Sportspun (50–gr. ball)—1 each white and pink. Size 5 knitting needles, OR SIZE REQUIRED TO OBTAIN GAUGE. Size 3 knitting needles. Velcro for back closing. 6 La Mode ½" red heart buttons.
GAUGE: 6 sts and 8 rows = 1".

BACKS: With smaller needles and pink, cast on 23 (25-27) sts. Work in k 1, p 1 rib for 5 rows. Change to larger needles and St st and work [4 rows white, 4 rows pink] 5 (6-6) times. Bind off.
FRONT: With smaller needles and pink, cast on 43 (49-55) sts and work in rib as for backs. Change to larger needles and work in color stripe and St st until first row of 4th (5th-5th) pink stripe is worked. Mark center 17 (19-21) sts. **Shape Neck:** Work to 1st marker, with 2nd strand of pink, p to next marker and sl to holder, p to end. Working each side separately and keeping to pat, dec 1 st at each neck edge on next row, then every other row 3 times more. Work even on 9 (11-14) sts until same length as back to shoulder. Bind off.
SLEEVES: With smaller needles and pink, cast on 35 (51-51) sts. Work rib as for backs. Change to larger needles and St st and, working in stripes as for back, inc 1 st each edge on first row, then every 4th row 4 times more. When 3" (3½"-4") from beg, bind off.
FINISHING: Sew shoulder seams. Centering sleeves at shoulder seams, sew in sleeves. Sew side and sleeve seams. **Neckband:** With smaller needles and pink, right side facing, beg at back neck edge, pick up and k about 71 (73-77) sts around neck edge, including sts from holder. Work in rib as for back for 5 rows. Bind off loosely. Right side facing, with smaller needles and pink, pick up and k about 34 (38-38) sts

along back edge; bind off. Work other back the same. Sew Velcro in place to close back. Sew hearts diagonally across front as shown in photo, with one heart on each stripe.

Boy's Heart Pullover

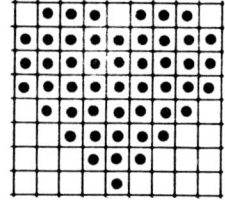

Heart

☐ Red
● White

Directions are for Small. Changes for Medium and Large are in parentheses.

MATERIALS: Bernat Berella Sportspun (50-gr. ball)—1 ball red and small amt. white. Size 5 knitting needles, OR SIZE REQUIRED TO OBTAIN GAUGE. 3 white 7/16" La Mode heart buttons. Velcro for back closing. Tapestry needle.
GAUGE: 6 sts and 8 rows = 1".

Using red throughout, work backs, front and sleeves as for Hearts and Stripes Sweater.
FINISHING: Mark center st of one sleeve, 1" from cast-on edge. With white, following chart in Figure 1, beg at marked st for bottom of heart, work heart in duplicate st as shown.
Finish as for Hearts and Stripes Sweater, sewing 3 buttons on front as shown in photograph, and using heart sleeve on side desired.

Child's Valentine Cardigan

Directions are for Size 2. Changes for Sizes 4, 6 and 8 are in parentheses.

MATERIALS: Bernat Berella "4" (3½-oz. ball)—1 (2-2-3) balls each red and white. Size G crochet hook, OR SIZE REQUIRED TO OBTAIN GAUGE. 6 white and 10 red ½" La Mode heart buttons. 6 red 7/16" La Mode heart buttons. Tapestry needle.
GAUGE: 4 dc = 1"; 5 rows = 2".

BACK: With red, ch 12. **Rib: Row 1:** Hdc in 2nd ch from hook and each rem ch. **Row 2:** Ch 1, turn; working in back lp only, hdc in each hdc—11 hdc. Rep Row 2 until 47 (51-55-59) rows from beg; do not fasten off. Turn work; working along ends of rows, ch 1, sc in end of each row—47 (51-55-59) sts. Ch 3 (counts as first dc), turn; dc in each st across. Work even in dc until 8" (9"-10"-11") or ½" less than desired length to underarm. Fasten off red. **Pat Row:** Join white; ch 3 for first dc, *work long dc in next st as follows:

yo, insert hook in same place as next st in row below and draw up lp to same height as last st, [yo, draw through 2 lps] twice; dc in next st; rep from * across. **Shape Armhole:** Turn; sl st in first 4 (4-6-6) sts, ch 3, work across in dc until 3 (3-5-5) sts rem; do not work in rem sts. Work even in white and dc until 4½" (5"-5¼"-5½") from beg of armhole. Fasten off.

LEFT FRONT: With red, work rib as for back for 23 (25-27-29) rows. Continue as for back on 23 (25-27-29) sts until Pat Row is completed.

Shape Armhole and Neck: Sl st in 4 (4-6-6) sts, ch 3, work in dc across—20 (22-22-25) sts. Work even until 2½" (2½"-3"-3") above beg of armhole; end at neck edge. Sl st in first 7 (8-9-10) sts, dc to end. Dec 1 st at neck edge every row 3 times. When same length as back to shoulder, fasten off.

RIGHT FRONT: Work as for left front, reversing shaping.

SLEEVES: Work rib as for back for 17 (19-21-23) rows. Fasten off red. Continue in white and dc, inc 1 st each edge every other row 10 (11-11-11) times. When sleeve measures 12½" (13½"-15"-16½") from beg, fasten off.

FINISHING: Sew shoulder seams; sew in sleeves, sewing sides of sleeves to armhole shaping. With tapestry needle, embroider a line of ch st across sleeve, at bottom of third-from-last row. Sew side and sleeve seams. **Front Bands and Neckband:** Beg at bottom of right front, work 1 row sc around to bottom of left front, taking care to keep work flat, and working 3 sc in top front corners. **Row 2:** Mark right front for 6 buttonholes evenly spaced with the first ½" from bottom and the last at neck corner. Ch 1, turn; sc in each sc, working corners as before, and working buttonholes opposite markers as follows: sc to marker, ch 1, sk 1 st, sc in next st. **Row 3:** Sc in each sc and ch around, working 3 sc in corner sc, and dec 3 sc around neck edge between corners. Sew buttons in place opposite buttonholes. Sew buttons scattered on both fronts and one sleeve as shown.

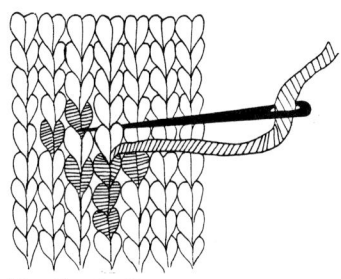
Duplicate St

Chain St

Doll's Valentine Cardigan

Directions are for Small. Changes for Medium and Large are in parentheses.

MATERIALS: Bernat Berella Sportspun (50–gr. ball)—1 ball each red and white. Size E crochet hook, OR SIZE REQUIRED TO OBTAIN GAUGE. 6 white and 9 red La Mode 7/16" heart buttons. Tapestry needle.
GAUGE: 5 dc = 1"; 5 rows = 2".

BACK: With red, ch 6. **Rib:** Row 1: Sc in 2nd ch from hook and each rem ch. Row 2: Ch 1, turn; working in back lp only, sc in each sc—5 sc. Rep Row 2 until 35 (41-45) rows from beg; do not fasten off. Turn work, working along ends of rows, ch 1, sc in each row—35 (41-45) sc. Ch 3 (counts as first dc), turn; dc in each rem st. Work even on 35 (41-45) dc until 5 (7-7) dc rows are completed. Fasten off red. **Pat Row:** Join white, ch 3 for first dc, *work long dc in next st as follows: yo, insert hook in same place as next st in row below and draw up lp to same height as last st, [yo and draw through 2 lps] twice; dc in next st; rep from * across. **Shape Armhole:** Turn; sl st in 5 sts, ch 3 (counts as first dc), work across in dc until 3 sts rem; do not work in rem sts. Continue in white on 29 (35-39) sts until 3" (4"-4") from beg of armhole. Fasten off.
LEFT FRONT: With red, ch 6 and work rib as for back for 17 (19-21) rows. Continue as for back on 17 (19-21) sts until Pat Row is completed. **Shape Armhole and Neck:** Sl st in 4 sts, ch 3, work in dc across—13 (15-19) sts. When 3" (5"-5") above beg of armhole shaping, end at neck edge. Sl st in first 5 (7-7) sts, dc to end. Dec 1 st at neck edge every row 2 times more. When same length as back to shoulder, fasten off.
RIGHT FRONT: Work as for left front, reversing shaping.
SLEEVES: With red, work rib as for back for 17 (27-27) rows. Fasten off red. Continue in white and dc, inc 1 st each edge every row 3 times. Work even until sleeve measures 4" (4½"-5") from beg. Fasten off.
FINISHING: Work as for Child's Valentine Cardigan.

VALENTINE DELIGHT
She loves me—she loves me not!
There's love to spare
in this happy group.

EASTER PARADE
Enjoy the fragrances of spring in parade-stopping finery.

BRAND-NEW-BABY: A PRECIOUS GIFT

Bringing baby home is a very special occasion.

SUMMER: TIME FOR FUN

Greet the good life—at the shore or on the courts—in these sporty outfits.

EASTER PARADE

Easter Outfit

Directions are for Small. Changes for Medium and Large are in parentheses.

MATERIALS: Chanteleine Sissi (50–gr. balls)—2 balls lilac and 1 ball white. Size F crochet hook, OR SIZE REQUIRED TO OBTAIN GAUGE. 3 ½" buttons. 1 yd. Offray hearts ribbon.

GAUGE: 3 V-st = 1".

DRESS

YOKE: Beg at neck edge with lilac, ch 52 (60-60). **Row 1:** Dc in 4th ch from hook and next 5 (6-6) ch, 3 dc in next ch for corner, dc in 11 (13-13) ch, 3 dc in next ch for 2nd corner, dc in 12 (14-14) ch, 3 dc in next ch for 3rd corner, dc in next 11 (13-13) ch, 3 dc in next ch, dc in next 6 (7-7) ch. **Row 2:** Ch 3 (counts as 1st dc), turn; dc in next 6 (7-7) dc, 3 dc in center dc of corner, dc in next 13 (15-15) dc, 3 dc in center dc of corner, dc in next 14 (16-16) dc, 3 dc in corner dc, dc in 13 (15-15) dc, 3 dc in corner dc, dc in 7 (8-8) dc. **Row 3:** Ch 3, turn; dc in 7 (8-8) dc for back, 3 dc in corner, dc in 15 (17-17) dc for sleeve, 3 dc in corner, dc in 16 (18-18) dc for front, 3 dc in corner, dc in 15 (17-17) dc for sleeve, 3 dc in corner, dc in 8 (9-9) dc for back. Work as for Row 3, having 1 more dc on each back and 2 more dc on each sleeve and front, 2 (2-3) times more—82 (90-98) sts. **Joining Row:** Ch 3, turn; dc in 10 (11-12) dc of back, 1 dc in corner dc, sk 21 (23-25) dc of sleeve, 1 dc in corner dc, dc in 22 (24-26) dc of front, 1 dc in corner dc, sk 21 (23-25) dc of sleeve, 1 dc in corner dc, dc in 11 (12-13) dc of back; join with sl st to 3rd ch of starting ch.

SKIRT: Row 1: Ch 4 (counts as 1 dc, ch 1), turn; dc in same dc, *[dc, ch 1, dc] all in next dc; rep from * across; join with sl st to 3rd ch of starting ch; sl st in ch–1 sp. **Row 2:** Ch 4, turn; dc in same sp, *[dc, ch 1, dc] all in next ch–1 sp of next V–st; rep from * around; join with sl st in 3rd ch of starting ch, sl st in ch–1 sp. Rep Row 2, 5 (5-7) times more. Fasten off.

FINISHING: Neck Edging: Right side facing, join white at left back neck edge, working along opposite side of turning ch, sc in each st around. Fasten off. **Sleeve:** Right side facing, join white at underarm, * sk ½" along edge, 5 dc in next st, sk about ½" along edge, sc in next st; rep from * around armhole, spacing so that 5 (6-7) shells are worked in all. Fasten off. Work other sleeve to correspond. Sew buttons in place to close back. Weave ribbon through first row of skirt and tie.

CAPE
With lilac, ch 54. **Row 1:** Dc in 4th ch from hook and each rem ch. **Row 2:** Ch 3, turn; dc in 2 sts; *2 dc in next st, dc in 3 sts; rep from * across; end last rep dc in 2 sts—64 sts. **Row 3:** Rep Row 2—80 sts. **Row 4:** Ch 3, turn, V–st in each st across; end dc in last st. **Row 5:** Ch 3, turn; *sk 1 st, V–st in next st; rep from * across; end dc in last dc. **Rows 6 and 7:** Rep Row 5. Fasten off lilac. **Row 8:** With white, *shell in V–st, sc between V–sts; repeat from * across; end sl st in last st. Fasten off.
FINISHING: Working along opposite side of ch at neck edge with white, sc in each ch. **Tie:** Ch 100; sl st in 2nd and each rem ch. Weave tie through first row of dc.

Sl st in 2nd and each rem chain

PURSE
With white, ch 4. **Rnd 1:** 11 dc in 4th ch from hook; join with sl st to 4th ch of starting ch. **Rnd 2:** Ch 3 (counts as 1 dc), dc in same st; *2dc in next st; rep from * around; join with sl st to starting ch. **Rnd 3:** Ch 3, dc in same st, dc in next st; *2 dc in next st, dc in next st; rep from * around—36 dc. Work 3 rows even. **Next Row (Beading Row):** Ch 4 (counts as 1 dc, ch 1), sk 1 dc, *dc in next dc, ch 1, sk 1 dc; rep from * around; join with sl st to 3rd ch of starting ch. Fasten off white; join lilac. **Edging:** Ch 4, turn; dc in same st, *sk 1 st, [dc, ch 1, dc] all in same st; rep from * around; join. **Last Rnd:** Rep Row 8 of Cape; join. Weave ribbon through beading row for purse strings.

Boy's Easter Suit

Directions are for Small. Changes for Medium and Large are in parentheses.

MATERIALS: Chanteleine Marly (50–gr. skein)—2 skeins blue. Size 7 knitting needles, OR SIZE REQUIRED TO OBTAIN GAUGE. Size 5 needles. 4 ¾" La Mode buttons. ½ yd. ½" elastic for waistband.
GAUGE: 5 sts and 7 rows = 1".

JACKET

BACK: With smaller needles, cast on 35 (40-45) sts. Work 8 rows Seed st. Change to larger needles and St st and work even until 4 ½" (5"-5½") from beg. Bind off.

RIGHT FRONT: With smaller needles, cast on 27 (31-33) sts. Work 8 rows Seed st. Continue in St st until 2" (2½"-2½") from beg; end with p row. **Shape Neck:** K 2 tog at beg of next row, then dec 1 st at front edge every row 14 (17-19) times more—12(13-13) sts. When same length as back to shoulder, bind off.

LEFT FRONT: Work as for right front, working buttonholes on 3rd and 14th rows as follows: From front edge, work 3 sts, yo, p 2 tog, work 7 sts, yo, p 2 tog, work to end of row. Complete to correspond to left front, reversing neck shaping.

SLEEVES: With smaller needles, cast on 29 (35-35) sts. Work in Seed st for 3 rows. Change to larger needles and St st, and work even until 2½" (3"-3½") from beg. Bind off.

FINISHING: Sew shoulder seams. Right side facing, with smaller needles, beg at right front bottom, pick up and k about 85 (105-115) sts around neck edge to left bottom edge. Bind off loosely. Centering sleeves at shoulder seams, sew in sleeves. Sew side and sleeve seams. Sew buttons opposite buttonholes.

PANTS

LEFT BACK: With smaller needles, cast on 21 (25-29) sts. Work 3 rows Seed st. Change to larger needles and St st, and work even until 1" from beg; end with p row. **Shape Crotch:** Bind off 2 (3-3) sts at beg of next row, then dec 1 st at same edge every other row 2 (3-3) times more—17 (19-23) sts. Work even until 2" (2½"-2½") above beg of crotch shaping. Change to smaller needles, and work in Seed st for ½". Bind off.

RIGHT BACK: Work as for left back, reversing shaping.

RIGHT FRONT: Work same as for left back. .

LEFT FRONT: Work as for right back.

FINISHING: Sew left and right backs together from waist to beg of crotch shaping. Sew left and right fronts tog from waist to crotch. Sew front to backs from bottom edge to crotch. Sew both side seams. Tack elastic to inside of waistband.

Flower-Trimmed Dress

Diagram 1

Directions are for Small. Changes for Medium and Large are in parentheses.

MATERIALS: Chanteleine Sonia (50–gr. ball)— 1 ball each green and yellow. Size 5 knitting needles, OR SIZE REQUIRED TO OBTAIN GAUGE. Size 3 needles. Size D crochet hook. Tapestry needle. 5 yellow ⅝" buttons, and 5 white ⅞" buttons, both La Mode style #160. Velcro for back closing.
GAUGE: 6 sts and 8 rows = 1".

BODICE BACKS: With larger needles, cast on 21 (23-27) sts. Work in St st until 3½" from beg. Bind off.
FRONT: With larger needles, cast on 43 (49-55) sts. Work in St st until 2" from beg. **Shape Neck:** Work 13 (15-17) sts, join 2nd strand of yarn and bind off next 17 (19-21) sts, work to end. Working each side separately, dec 1 st at each neck edge every other row 3 times—10 (12-15) sts. When same length as backs to shoulder, bind off.
SLEEVES: With smaller needles and green, cast on 41 (57-57) sts. Work in Seed st for 3 rows. Change to larger needles and St st. When 3" (3½"-4") from beg, bind off. Sew shoulder seams. Right side facing, with green, pick up and k about 65 (69-73) sts around neck edge, and work in Seed st for 3 rows. Bind off loosely in pat. Sew side seams ½" from bottom edge. Sew sleeve seams; sew in sleeves, gathering fullness at top.
SKIRT: Right side facing, with larger needles and green, pick up and k 85 (95-109) sts along bottom edge of bodice. **Row 1:** K 1, p 1 in each st across—170 (190-218) sts. Work even in St st until 2" from beg. Fasten off green. With yellow, continue in St st for 2" more. Fasten off yellow. With Green, work 4 rows Seed st. Fasten off.
FINISHING: Sew back skirt seam. **Embroidery:** Sew five flowers evenly spaced across front in yellow band as shown in Diagram 1 as follows: Place yellow button over white button; holding them tog, sew in place. With green, work 1 straight for stem, and 2 lazy-daisy sts for leaves.

Springtime Pinafore

Directions are given for Small. Changes for Medium and Large are in parentheses.

MATERIALS: Chanteleine Sonia (50–gr. ball)—1 each pink and white. Size 5 knitting needles, OR SIZE REQUIRED TO OBTAIN GAUGE. Size 3 needles. Size D crochet hook. 1 yd. matching ¾" ribbon. 5 purple ¾" buttons, La Mode style #160. Velcro for back closing and strap fastening. **GAUGE:** 6 sts and 8 rows = 1".

SKIRT: With pink, work as for Doll's Pinafore, page 12, until seams are sewn. Wrong side facing, with smaller needles, sl sts from holder. With pink, k 2 tog across. Continue in garter st for 3 rows more (2 ridges on right side). Right side facing, change to white and St st and work 1"; fasten off white. With pink, work 4 rows garter st; bind off loosely. **Straps:** Cast on 7 sts. Work even in St st for 6" (7"-7"). Bind off. Sew straps to ribbon and sew to front. Work 1 row sc along each side of back opening. Sew Velcro in place to close back and fasten straps. Sew 5 buttons across front.

BRINGING HOME BABY

Christening Gown

Directions are for Small. Changes for Medium and Large are in parentheses.

MATERIALS: Coats & Clark Red Heart Baby Yarn (2–oz. skein)—2 skeins white. Blanket (not shown): 2 skeins. Size 3 knitting needles, OR SIZE REQUIRED TO OBTAIN GAUGE. 3 yd. ½" Offray white double-faced satin ribbon. Small amt. white hat elastic.
GAUGE: 15 sts = 2"; 10 rows = 1".

DRESS
BODY: Beg at bottom edge, cast on 121 (161-201) sts. K 2 rows. **Pat Row 1 (right side):** K 1, *k 2 tog, k 7, yo, k 1, yo, k 7, k 2 tog, k 1; rep from * across. **Row 2:** K. **Row 3:** Rep Row 1. **Row 4:** P. Rep Rows 3 and 4 until 12" (14"-16") from beg; end right side row. **Shape Bodice:** K 4 (1-4), *k 2 tog, k 5 (2-1); rep from * across; end last rep k 3 (2-3)—104 (121-136) sts. K 2 more rows. **Beading Row:** K 1, * k 2 tog, k 2; rep from * across; end last rep k 2 (1-2). K 4 more

rows; dec 0 (1-0) st at end of last row. **Divide for Backs and Front:** K 22 (26-30) and sl to holder for right back, bind off 8 sts, k 44 (52-60) and sl to holder for front; bind off 8 sts, k to end. Work even in St st on 22 (26-30) sts until 2½" (3"-3") from beg. Bind off. Wrong side facing, sl sts for right back to needle and work to correspond. Wrong side facing, sl sts for front to needle and work even in St st until 1" less than backs to shoulder; end with p row. **Shape Neck:** K 10 (12-15) sts, with new strand of yarn, bind off next 24 (28-30) sts, k to end. Working each side separately, dec 1 st each neck edge every row 4 times. When same length as back to shoulder, bind off.

SLEEVES: Cast on 48 (60-60) sts. **Border:** K 4 rows. **Beading Row:** K 1, *yo, k 2 tog, k 2; rep from * across; end last rep k 1. K 3 more rows. Continue in St st until 3" (3½"-3½"); bind off.

FINISHING: Sew shoulder seams. Right side facing, beg at back neck edge, pick up and k about 80 (84-88) sts around neck edge. K 3 rows. Work Beading Row as for sleeve. K 3 more rows; bind off. Sew in sleeves, sewing sides of sleeve to bound-off sts, and making an inverted pleat at shoulder seam. Sew back. Weave ribbon through waist, neck and sleeve beading.

BONNET

Cast on 60 (72-80) sts and work as for sleeve border. Keeping 4 sts at each edge in garter st, continue in St st until 2½" (3"-3½") from beg. Bind off 20 (24-26) sts at beg of next 2 rows. Work even until 2½" (2½"-2¾") from bind off. Work 4 rows garter st. Bind off. Sew bound-off edges to sides of back. Weave ribbon through front edge.

BOOTIES

Cast on 44 (48-52) sts. Work 8 rows as for sleeve border. Continue in St st until 4" (4½"-4½") from beg; end with p row. **Shape Toe:** *K 2 tog, k 2; rep from * across. P 1 row. **Row 3:** *K 2 tog, k 1; rep from * across. P 1 row. **Row 5:** K 2 tog across. Rep last 2 rows once—6 (6-7) sts. Cut yarn, leaving a 12" end. Thread through rem sts and fasten securely. Sew back seam. Weave hat elastic through about 1" from top and secure. Weave ribbon through top beading row.

BLANKET (not shown)

Cast on 169 sts. Keeping 4 sts each edge in garter st throughout, work in pat as for body of medium-sized dress on center 161 sts until about 24" from beg. Rep Rows 1 and 2; k 2 rows. Bind off.

Layette

Directions are for Small. Changes for Medium and Large are in parentheses.

MATERIALS: Coats & Clark Red Heart Baby Yarn (2–oz. skein)—2 skeins each Pastel Green and Peach. Size E crochet hook, OR SIZE REQUIRED TO OBTAIN GAUGE. 2 buttons.
GAUGE: 6 hdc and 4 rows = 1″.

NOTE: Hdc are worked in back lp only unless otherwise stated.

DRESS

Beg at bottom edge, ch 110 (122-134). **Row 1:** With green, hdc in 2nd ch from hook and next 6 (7-8) ch, *3 hdc in next ch, hdc in next 6 (7-8) ch, sk 2 ch, hdc in next 6 (7-8) ch; rep from * across; end hdc in next 6 (7-8) ch, dec 1 hdc over next 2 ch. **Row 2:** Ch 1, turn; hdc in 2nd st, hdc in next 6 (7-8) hdc; *3 hdc in next st, hdc in next 6 (7-8) hdc, sk 2 sts, hdc in next 6 (7-8) hdc; rep from * across; end hdc in 6 (7-8) hdc, dec 1 st over last 2 sts. **Row 3:** With peach, rep Row 2. **Row 4:** Rep Row 2. Continue as for Row 2, working 2 rows green and 2 rows peach, until 4th peach row is worked. Work 1 more row green. **Next Row:** Working through both lps, ch 5, turn; sk 0 (1-2) sts, *tr in next st, sk 1 st, dc in next st, sk 1 st, hdc in next st, sk 1 st, sc in next st, sk 1 st, sc in next st, sk 1 st, hdc in next st, sk 1 st, dc in next st, sk 1 st, tr in next st, sk 0 (1-2) sts, tr in next 2 sts, sk next 0 (1-2) sts; repeat from * across; end last rep sk 0 (1-2) sts, tr in last st. Ch 1, turn; sc in each st. Fasten off green.
Shape Bodice: Mark center 17 (21-25) sts. Join green in first marked st, working through both lps, hdc to next marked st. Work even in hdc, working through both lps, on 17 (21-25) sts until 8 rows are completed. **Shape Straps:** Ch 3 (counts as first dc), dc in next 3 dc. Work even in dc on 4 sts until 3″ (3½″-4″) long. Fasten off. Join yarn in 4th st from end of last bodice row worked; work to correspond to first strap.
FINISHING: Sew back seam. With peach, beg at center back, work 1 row sc around entire top edge, taking care to keep work flat. Fasten off. Sew 2 buttons to back to fasten straps.

BONNET

With green, ch 81. Work in pat as for medium-sized dress until 2nd green stripe is completed. Fasten off. Fold in half. Sew first and last 9 sts tog; sew corresponding 9 sts at fold tog; sew back seam. **Center Motif:** Beg at seam, work 1 row hdc around opening. Working in spiral, not joining rnds, sc in every other st until 5 sts rem; draw up a lp in each of last 5 sts, yo and through all lps on hook. **Ties:** With green, ch 66. Sc in 2nd and each ch, 3 sc in last ch, working along opposite side of ch, sc in each st. Fasten off.

BOOTIES
With green, ch 35; join with sl st to form ring. Ch 2 (counts as first hdc), turn; hdc in each rem st; join with sl st to 2nd ch of starting ch. Rep this row 6 times more. Fasten off.
FINISHING: Fold in half with joining at back. Sew bottom seam. Sew 3 sts of top tog for instep. **Edging:** Join peach at center back; ch 2, hdc in same st, *hdc in next 2 sts, 2 sc in next st; rep from * around; end 2 hdc in last st—40 sts. **Last Row:** Ch 2, sk 2 sts; *hdc in 2 sts, 3 hdc in next st, hdc in 2 sts, sk 2 sts; rep from * around; end last rep hdc in 1 st; join with sl st to 2nd ch of starting ch. Fasten off. **Ties:** Ch 12″. Sl st in 2nd and each rem ch. Fasten off. Weave through first peach row.

BLANKET
With green, ch 122 and work as for medium-sized dress until about 24″ fom beg; end with green stripe. Fasten off. Working along ends of rows, work 1 row sc along each side edge.

SUMMER: TIME FOR FUN

Sailor Girl and Sailor Boy

Directions are for Small. Changes for Medium and Large are in parentheses.

MATERIALS: Plymouth Emu Superwash DK (50–gr. ball)—2 balls blue and 1 white for each. Size 5 knitting needles, OR SIZE REQUIRED TO OBTAIN GAUGE. Size 3 needles. ½ yd. Offray ribbon #5161. Velcro for back closing. 1 yd. ½″ elastic for waistbands.
GAUGE: 6 sts and 8 rows = 1″.

SKIRT
With blue, work as skirt of Doll's Pinafore, page 12, until seams are sewn.
FINISHING: Right side facing, sl sts to smaller needle and work in k 1, p 1 rib for ½″. Bind off. Sew elastic in place.

SHORTS
LEFT BACK: With smaller needles and blue, cast on 25 (29-33) sts. Work 3 rows Seed st. Continue in St st on larger needles until 1½" from beg; end with p row. **Shape Crotch:** Bind off 2 sts at beg of next row, then dec 1 st at same edge every other row 2 (3-4) times. Work even until 4½" from beg of crotch. With smaller needles, work k 1, p 1 rib for ½". Bind off.
RIGHT BACK: Work as for left back, reversing shaping.
RIGHT FRONT: Work as for left back.
LEFT FRONT: Work as for right back.
FINISHING: Sew fronts tog from top to crotch; sew backs the same; sew fronts to backs from bottom edge to crotch; sew side seams. Sew elastic in place.

GIRL'S OR BOY'S TOP
BACKS AND SLEEVES: With blue, work as for Hearts and Stripes Sweater, working 5 rows Seed st instead of bottom rib.
FRONT: With smaller needles and blue, cast on 43 (49-55) sts; work 5 rows Seed st. Continue in St st on larger needles until 2" from beg; end p row. **Yoke:** K 21 (24-27), p 1, k to end. **Next Row:** P 20 (23-26), k 1, p 1, k 1, p to end. Continue in St st, working 2 more st at center in Seed st until 4" from beg. **Shape Neck:** Work to Seed st, with 2nd strand of blue, bind off all Seed sts, work to end. Working each side separately, dec 1 st each neck edge every other row until 9 (11-14) sts rem. When same length as backs; bind off.
FINISHING: Sew shoulders; sew in sleeves; sew side and sleeve seams. **Left Collar:** With smaller needles and white, cast on 44 (48-52) sts. Work in garter st for 19 rows. **Next Row:** Bind off 30 (32-34) sts; k to end. Work even on rem sts for 1½" (2"-2") or until long enough to fit back neck; bind off. Work right collar to correspond, reversing shaping by binding off on Row 21.
Sew ribbon in place along top edge of yoke. Sew collars in place. Sew Velcro in place to close.

Tennis Outfit

Directions are for Small. Changes for Medium and Large are in parentheses.

MATERIALS: Plymouth Emu DK (50–gr. ball)—2 balls white, 1 ball aqua, small amt. red.

Size 5 knitting needles, OR SIZE REQUIRED TO OBTAIN GAUGE. Size 3 needles. Size D crochet hook. Velcro for back closing.
GAUGE: 6 sts and 8 rows = 1".

SWEATER

BACKS: Working as for Hearts and Stripes Sweater, page 37, work 2 rows red and 3 rows aqua rib. Continue in white and St st until 6" (6½"-6½") from beg; bind off.

FRONT: With smaller needles and red, cast on 46 (50-54) sts. Work rib as for backs. **Row 1:** K 4 (6-8) sts, [p 2, k 4, p 2, k 7] twice, p 2, k to end. **Rows 2 and 4:** K the k sts and p the p sts as they face you. **Row 3 (Cable Row):** K 4 (6-8) sts, [p 2, cable: sl next 2 sts to cable needle and hold in back, k next 2 sts, k 2 sts from cable needle; p 2, k 7] twice, p 2, cable, p 2, k to end. Rep these 4 rows 3 times. **Divide for Neck:** Work 21 (23-25) sts in pat, with 2nd strand of white, bind off 4 sts, work pat to end. Discontinuing pats as needed, dec 1 st each neck edge every row 11 (12-13) times. When same length as backs, bind off.

SLEEVES: With smaller needles and red, cast on 37 (53-53) sts; work rib as for front. **Next Row:** P 1, *k 2, p 1; rep from * across. **Row 2:** K 1, *p 2, k 1; rep from * across. Rep these 2 rows until 3" (3½"-3½") from beg. Bind off.

FINISHING: Sew shoulders. **Neckband:** Right side facing, with smaller needles and aqua, pick up and k about 61 (65-71) sts around neck edge. Work k 1, p 1 rib for 2 rows aqua and 2 rows red; bind off loosely. Sew in sleeves; sew side and sleeve seams. With white, work 1 row sc along each back edge. Sew Velcro in place to close.

SHORTS
With aqua, work as for Sailor Boy, page 57.

Jogging Suit

Directions are for Small. Changes for Medium and Large are in parentheses.

MATERIALS: Plymouth Emu DK (50–gr. ball)—2 balls yellow, 1 oz. each red and aqua. Size 5 knittting needles, OR SIZE REQUIRED TO OBTAIN GAUGE. Size 3 needles. Size D crochet hook. Velcro for back closing. ½ yd. ½" elastic for waist.
GAUGE: 6 sts and 8 rows = 1".

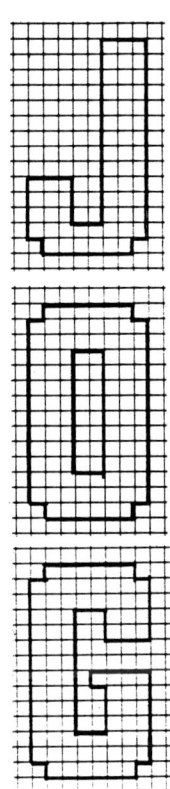

PANTS
LEFT BACK: With smaller needles and yellow, cast on 25 (29-33) sts. Work 5 rows k 1, p 1 rib. Change to larger needles and work even in St st until 4½" (5"-5") from beg. Complete as for left back of Sailor Boy's Shorts.
RIGHT BACK: Work as for left back, reversing crotch shaping.
RIGHT FRONT: Work as for left back.
LEFT FRONT: Work as for right back.
Finish as for Sailor Boy's Shorts.

SWEATER
BACKS AND SLEEVES: With yellow, work as for Hearts and Stripes Sweater.
FRONT: With yellow, work as for Hearts and Stripes Sweater until rib is completed, inc 1 st at end of last row—44 (50-56) sts. Continue in St st on larger needles until 2" (2½"-2½") from beg; end p row. **Next Row (right side):** Mark center 28 sts.
Work to first marker; following first row of chart for "G", k 1 yellow, 6 red, 1 yellow; k 2 yellow; follow chart for "O"; k 2 yellow; follow chart for "J"; k in yellow to end. Continue in St st, following charts, working letters with 1 row more red, 2 rows aqua, 2 rows red 3 times more, and carrying colors not in use loosely across back of work. When 1" less than backs to shoulders, end p row. **Shape Neck:** Mark center 20 (22-24) sts. Work to first marker, with 2nd ball of yellow, bind off to next marker, work to end. Working each side separately, dec 1 st each edge every other row 3 times. When same length as backs, bind off.
FINISHING: With yellow, finish as for Hearts and Stripes Sweater.

MIX AND MATCH

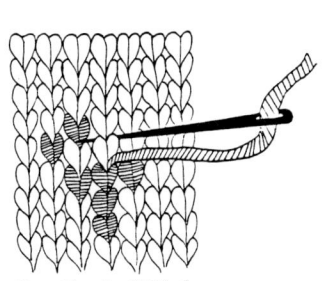

Duplicate Stitch

For the book's last sweaters, we have given you an endless variety of new beginnings—sweaters like the Rose Sweaters we made, with a choice of 11 other charts.

We have used the same pattern and materials used in the Scottie Sweaters, page 9 and 10, but we used blue throughout (in the same yarn amounts as yellow for the Scottie Sweaters).

After these sweaters were knit, the roses were then worked in duplicate stitch, following the rose chart. Any of the 11 other charts, can be substituted for the rose. Because the child's

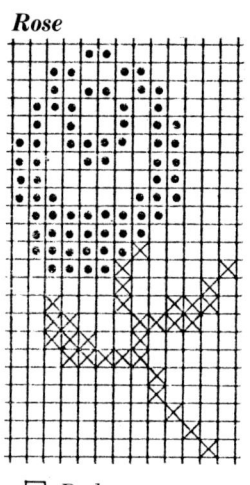

Rose

● Red
☒ Green

sweater is made in worsted-weight yarn and the doll's sweater is made in sport weight, the same chart can be used on both, and the design will be proportionally smaller on the doll's finer gauge sweater.

To place the design, count the number of stitches wide and high on the chart—the rose is 12 sts wide by 23 sts high. With a running stitch, mark an area on the front of the sweater which is that number of stitches wide and high. Then, duplicate stitch as shown at left.

You can also adapt your own needlepoint or filet crochet charts. The only trick is to elongate the chart by about one-fourth, since in needlepoint or filet crochet, there are about the same number of stitches and rows per inch, but in knitting there are about one-forth more rows than stitches to the inch, depending on gauge.

We are sure you can think of even more variations!

RESOURCES

If you have any difficulty finding materials used in this book, contact the company below for ordering information.

Susan Bates Inc
Rt 9A
Chester, CT 06412

Bernat Yarn and Craft Corp.
Uxbridge, MA 01569

Bucilla
Order Entry Department
Armour Handcrafts, Inc.
Valmont Industrial Park
Jaycee Drive
West Hazelton, PA 18201

Coats & Clark, Inc.
Department CS
P.O. Box 1010
Toccoa, GA 30577

CM Offray & Son, Inc.
Rt 24, Box 601
Chester, NJ

Crystal Palace Yarns
Chanleleine Yarns
3006 San Pablo Avenue
Berkeley, CA 94702

Joseph Galler
27 West 20th St.
New York, NY 10011

La Mode Buttons
140 Kero Road
Carlstadt, NJ 07072

Pingouin
P.O. Box 100
Jamestown, SC 29453

Plymouth Yarn Company
500 Lafayette St.
Bristol, PA 19007

Velcro USA
406 Brown Ave.
Manchester, NH 03108

Wright's Mill Store
South Street
West Warren, MA 01092

HOW TO KNIT

CASTING ON

Allow 1″ of yarn for each stitch. Then make a slip loop as shown, with the measured end at left and "working" or ball end at right.

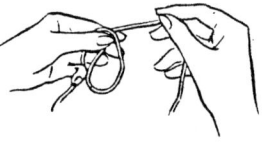

Turn loop as shown, so ball end is behind loop. Put the needle behind the loose end of yarn and pull through; tighten loop.

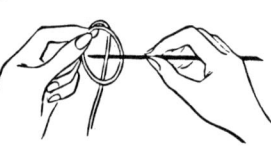

This is how to hold the loose end of yarn in your left hand. The needle is ready to be slipped under the yarn around your thumb.

With the ball end of the yarn in right hand, put needle under strand that circles thumb. With right index finger, slip yarn in back of needle. (You now have knotted loop around thumb.) Slip this loop over end of needle. Pull both ends gently but firmly to tighten loop.

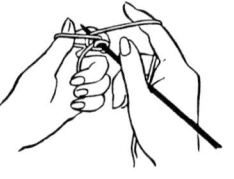

Continue to cast on stitches until you have the desired number.

This shows how to hold your hands while knitting.

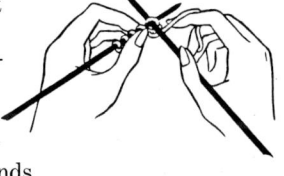

KNIT STITCH (k)

Hold needle with stitches (sts) in left hand. Take your other needle and slip it through the first loop (lp) as shown, from the front towards the back.

Take the ball end of the yarn with your right index finger and bring it around the back of the right needle towards you.

Holding the yarn firmly with your right index finger, use your right needle to bring the new lp you have just made through the first st on the left needle. Sl that st completely off the left needle.

This is your first k st. Knit all remaining sts; your work will be entirely on your right needle. Take that needle in your left hand and the empty needle in your right hand.

Now work the next row.

PURL STITCH (p)

Slip your right needle through the first lp as shown, from the back to the front.

Pass the ball end of the yarn back between the V made by the points of the needles; pass it around the point of the right needle as shown.

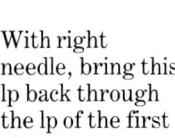

With right needle, bring this lp back through the lp of the first st.

Slide st off left needle. This is your first p st. P all remaining sts; your work will be entirely on your right needle. Take that needle in your left hand and the empty needle in your right.

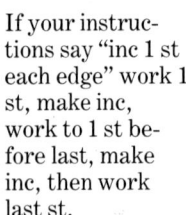

INCREASING (inc)

Work to where the inc is to be made. Sl the strand between the st just worked and next st by inserting right needle under this strand as if to p, twisting it, and placing it on left needle; k this lp.

If your instructions say "inc 1 st each edge" work 1 st, make inc, work to 1 st before last, make inc, then work last st.

DECREASING (dec)

There are 2 ways of dec, each used in a specific way.

For the dec to slant from left to right, insert right needle from the front, through the front lps of 2 sts, then k to form these sts into a single st.

For the dec to slant from right to left, sl 1 st inserting the needle from back to front.
K the next st.

Then slip the slipped st over the st just k. This is often called SKP.

BINDING OFF

Work 2 sts; take left needle and pick up the lp of the first st, pass it over the 2nd st but do not pull too tightly.

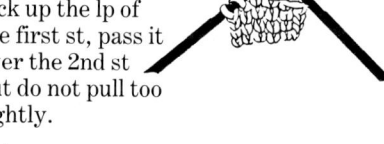

PICKING UP STITCHES

When you have finished a sweater and have to work the neckband, with the right side facing, join yarn at shoulder seam, put the right needle through the double lp at the end of next row as shown, yo as to knit, bring lp through—you now have 1 st on needle.

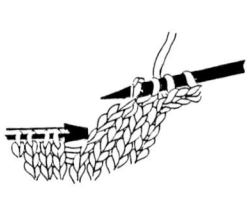

Continue in this manner around the neck. If there are sts on holders, k across those sts.

HOW TO CROCHET

BEGINNINGS
Start a slip loop with short end at left, and "working" or ball end at right.

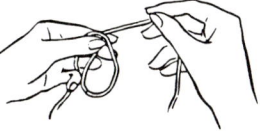

Hold hook in right hand as you would a pencil, with middle finger near tip as shown.

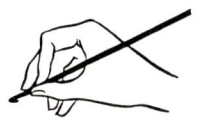

Turn loop so working end is behind loop. Put hook through loop and behind working end. Draw loop through, and tighten.

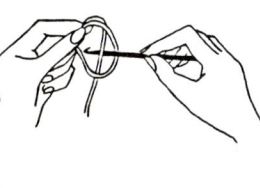

This is how to hold your yarn to keep the tension right.

To begin work, adjust finger as shown. Bend the middle finger to regulate tension, but keep yarn from moving too freely with ring and little fingers.

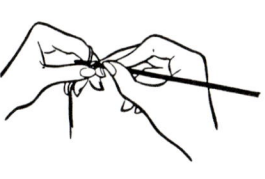

CHAIN STITCH (ch st)
Catch yarn as shown; draw through loop (lp) on hook. Do not draw too tightly—you have to be able to put your hook through this stitch later.

Repeat this until you have as many ch as you need, with 1 always staying on hook. Practice until sts are even.

SINGLE CROCHET (sc)
To begin first row, insert hook as shown in 2nd ch from hook.

Wrap yarn over (yo) hook as shown.

Draw lp through.

There are now 2 lps on hook. Yo and draw lp through.

Sc is completed.

Repeat this until you have worked 1 sc in each ch st. Ch 1 at end of row to turn.

Working through both lps of each sc, work until required number of rows are completed. To fasten off, cut yarn. Leaving a 4" end. Pull end through last lp.

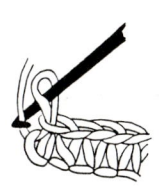

HALF DOUBLE CROCHET (hdc)

Yo hook; insert hook into 3rd ch from hook and draw up a lp.

Yo and draw lp through all 3 lps on hook. Repeat until you have worked 1 hdc in each ch.

Ch 2 at end of row to turn. Work hdc in each hdc. Work until required number of rows are completed.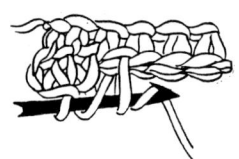

DOUBLE CROCHET (dc)

Yo hook; insert hook into 4th ch from hook and draw up a lp.

Yo and draw lp through 2 lps; two lps remain on hook.

Yo and draw lp through 2 lps. Dc is completed. Repeat until you have worked 1 dc in each ch.

Ch 3 at end of row to turn. This is usually counted as the first dc of the row.

Working through both lps of each dc, work until required number of rows are completed. Fasten off as for sc.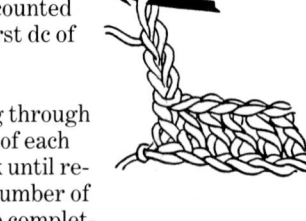

TRIPLE CROCHET (tr)

Yo hook twice; insert hook into 5th ch from hook; then [yo and draw through 2 lps] 3 times. Tr is completed. Ch 4 to turn row.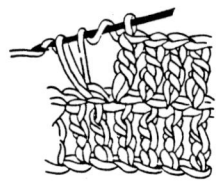

To increase (all sts): Work 2 sts in 1 st.

To decrease in Sc: Draw up a lp in 2 sts, yo and through all lps on hook.

To decrease in Hdc: Yo and draw up a lp in 1 st, draw up a lp in next st; yo and through all lps on hook.

To decrease in dc: Yo and draw up a lp in 1 st, yo and draw lp through 2 lps on hook, yo and draw up a lp in next st, yo and draw t through 2 lps on hook, yo and draw through rem 3 lps.